PARISH LIFE
UNDER QUEEN ELIZABETH

ROEHAMPTON :

PRINTED BY JOHN GRIFFIN.

PARISH LIFE
UNDER QUEEN ELIZABETH

AN INTRODUCTORY STUDY

BY

W. P. M. KENNEDY, M.A.,

PROFESSOR OF MODERN HISTORY IN THE UNIVERSITY OF
ST. FRANCIS XAVIER'S COLLEGE, ANTIGONISH,
NOVA SCOTIA

LONDON:

THE MANRESA PRESS, ROEHAMPTON, S.W.
B. HERDER, 68, GREAT RUSSELL STREET, W.C.

1914

Nihil Obstat:

S. GEORGIUS KIERAN HYLAND, S.T.D.,
CENSOR DEPUTATUS

Imprimatur:

✠ PETRUS, EPŨS. SOUTHWARC.

TO

S. J. C.

12 October, 1913.

PREFACE.

BEFORE entering on the study of Elizabethan Parish Life, it is well to recall that, from Thomas Cromwell's general visitation of the parishes of England in 1536 down to the death of Mary, the people had been tossed about in the eddies of religious change. At one time it was semi-Catholicism, at another Protestantism—in varying degrees—at another Catholicism. They felt the ebb and flow of the different positions taken up by the rulers, and their lives for a quarter of a century had been passing through a ceaseless variety of religious experience. This fact has an important bearing on Elizabethan life. Men did not know how soon they would be forced to shift their positions, and hence there was abroad great uneasiness and little stability. A generation brought up in an atmosphere of religious movements, and dragooned from one religious camp to another, was hardly likely to know what to do, or say, or believe. There was no security that their acceptance of a new state of affairs to-day would be pleasing to the government to-morrow. This instability and lack of certainty produced a wide spirit of moral weakness which is too often forgotten in studying Elizabethan England. It only gradually dawned on the nation that the government had a religious policy, and that it was worth while to accept it. The strong men in reality were the conscientious Puritans and Catholics, who had the courage to refuse a position which gradually made itself secure.

My object in this little book is to present a broad picture of Elizabethan life. I have called it "an Introductory Study," as it would require a larger volume than this to deal with the details of such a complicated subject. The book is intended for the general reader, who may wish to know something of how the Elizabethan Reformation affected the every-day life of the people. As there is so much in dispute, I have thought it best to add references, and these may be of some aid to students of the period. In addition, they will serve to give some support to my positions and to clear the air amid the dust of controversy. I have done my best to eliminate prejudice.

It would be impossible for me to acknowledge in detail all that I owe to the older historians of the reign. I would, however, express my indebtedness to Professor Pollard, Dr. Frere, Dr. Gee, and Father Birt, O.S.B., whose writings have passed into the common heritage of Tudor history. The materials on which I have worked were collected many years ago. Writing as I now do, far from originals and the large libraries, I have had to make use of my note-books on the documents, &c. Thus as a rule I have been compelled to give references to much material which I am conscious is more accessible than my notes imply.   I can only ask my critics to remember the circumstances under which I write and to deal kindly with the notes.

I owe sincere thanks to my colleague, Dr. Hugh MacPherson, for encouragement and help as the book progressed; to Mr. Joseph Wall, K.C., for generously giving me of his time and knowledge, and for reading my manuscript.   I would also desire to thank the Editor of " The Catholic Library " for all the kindness which he has extended to me as this little book went through the press.

W. P. M. KENNEDY.

The University of St. Francis Xavier's,
Antigonish, Nova Scotia.
January 24, 1914.

CONTENTS.

CHAPTER I.

THE PRELUDES OF CHANGE.

PARISH Life implies authority, whether civil or ecclesiastical. Changes and fluctuations do not come about in the every-day life of a parish without some power behind which has usurped or been given authority to bring them about. An Act of Parliament may transform a whole country, the bye-laws of a local body may change the face of an entire neighbourhood, and the inhabitants may thus find themselves gradually drawn away from the traditions of the past, or whirled about in the eddies of varied movements as authority flits from one position to another. At times a new authority lays down clear-cut lines of action at the very beginning of its régime, as it did under Queen Elizabeth, and the people are slowly drawn within the new influences; or at times it moves from point to point of change as it did under Edward VI, and the people share in the unenviable life of its instability and insecurity,—their lives reflect its life. Thus then it is necessary, if any adequate idea of parish life during any period is to be obtained, to know in some detail the changes produced by authority, and in a lesser degree to understand some of the motives under whose influence authority has acted. The broad outlines of history must necessarily form an introduction to the subject, for parish life is to a large extent the application of this history to national life. There may be local

B

modifications, and local divergences, but, broadly
speaking, the study of parish life can best be ap-
proached by a review of the general action of
authority during the period. In many cases this
is a difficult and complicated work, for the authority at work comes at times into contact with
influences which bring to it the elements of a waver-
ing policy. On the other hand the study of parish
life under Queen Elizabeth is rendered easier by
the fact that authority in the earlier months of the
reign laid foundations which were permanent
throughout the period, and on which were built
at various times structures admirably in keeping
with these foundations. It will be necessary then
to turn to these earlier months, and to review in
some detail the changes made by authority, round
which gather the changes made in parochial and
diocesan life. Further authoritative changes come
at definite periods and in definite groups, and these
will be considered later in their proper connexion;
but they in no way contract the work of the beginning of the reign—they rather amplify and supple-
ment it. There is consistency in Elizabeth's policy
in so far as it affected parish life.

Archbishop Pole died on Nov. 17, 1558,[1] the
same day as Queen Mary, and during the ensuing
thirteen months events took place which had a lasting influence on the nation. The legislation and
changes of these months lie behind the parish life
of the entire reign, and it will be necessary to form
a fairly full conception of the ecclesiastical system

[1] There is some difficulty about the date of Pole's death.
Wriothesley dates it Nov. 15; Machyn, Nov. 19. I have
followed *The Venetian Calendar*.

erected by Elizabeth and her advisers—bishops, statesmen, lords and commons. We are not here concerned with the rights or wrongs of this system, we study it only in connexion with parochial life. To weigh it in its relation to Catholicism would carry us too far afield, and in addition the subject has been fully treated within recent years by Catholic historians, whose work leaves little place for further elaboration.[1]

Queen Mary's national legacy to her successor was full of ambiguities and difficulties. Financial affairs were in a precarious state and trade was in a deplorable position. There was no Primate at a moment when the Church in England emphatically needed a guiding hand. Five of the bishoprics were vacant, and within a short period death was to render vacant five more sees.[2] The war with France had not been brought to a conclusion, and foreign affairs were complicated by the fact that Mary Queen of Scotland had married the Dauphin, and had thus welded together the old antipathies of these two nations against England. A contemporary State paper[3] says that " the Commonwealth was diseased by the poverty of the Queen; the penury of noblemen and their poverty; the wealth of the meaner sort; the dearth of things; the divisions within the realm; the wars; want of justice . . . the Queen poor; the realm

<hr />

[1] See Rev. G. E. Phillips, *The Extinction of the Ancient Hierarchy* (1905); Dom Birt, *The Elizabethan Religious Settlement* (1907).

[2] See Stubbs, *Registrum Sacrum Anglicanum* (1897); and *The Venetian Calendar* (1558-1580), p. 105.

[3] *State Papers Domestic Eliz.* i. 66.

exhausted; the nobility poor and decayed; want of good captains and soldiers; the people out of order; justice not executed; all things dear; excess in meat, drink and apparel; division among ourselves; wars with France and Scotland; the French king bestriding the realm, having one foot in Calais and the other in Scotland; steadfast enmity but no steadfast friendship abroad." An awkward friendship with Spain marked the opening of the reign, foretaste of that time-serving diplomacy which during her life stood Elizabeth in good stead. Philip was thus conciliated, perhaps by being led to hope for the Queen's hand, and Feria, his ambassador in England, successfully urged him to use his influence with Paul IV to prevent anything rash being done at Rome with regard to her.[1]

The foreign ambassadors watched with anxiety every move on the part of the new Queen, who however gave them little to go upon. With regard to her personal religion she equivocated as often as it suited her. If it helped her position, she rapturously kissed a Bible in public while she played with Catholic ceremonial in her chapel. If she had any religious convictions she kept them for the recesses of her private life, and to all questions in this connexion she replied by ambiguous actions and doubtful words. She called at once into her service William Cecil, who, like herself, had conformed to Catholicism under Mary, and who showed from the very beginning of his public life

[1] See F. W. Maitland, *Collected Papers*, iii. pp. 165 ff., and *English Historical Review*, xv. 324.

a diplomacy and tact characterized, like that of his sovereign, by duplicity and double-dealing. When Feria wrote to his master that Elizabeth "has not hitherto been a Catholic," he summed up clearly the religious position of Cecil as well. Both he and Elizabeth had conformed for policy, and policy was destined to be their guide in the future as in the past. Quiet and unobtrusive changes took place in the Council. Thus, when her reign was scarcely a month old, we find that no less than eleven old members were summoned to its meetings, and the future changes among her advisers were carried out gradually and with enough discrimination to prevent any severe difficulties in carrying on the government of the country. In foreign affairs, the conciliation of Philip made it clear that for the present at least he could be relied on to oppose France, and Paul IV held his hand in deference to the Spanish monarch. Thus, while Elizabeth's foreign affairs in a manner solved themselves, the internal and thorny religious problem at home was rendered less complicated by the absence of any pronouncement against her from the Pope, and of any fear of a Spanish war. A Royal Proclamation[1] forbade the use of "any other manner of public prayer, rite, or ceremony in the church but that which is already used and by law received." All preaching was for the present silenced. Hints of change were however conveyed in the document, which promised that Parliament would be consulted shortly "in matters and cere-

---

[1] December 27, 1558. Gee and Hardy, *Documents*, No. lxxvii.

monies of religion." Dr. Bill, a mild and innocuous preacher, preached a "goodly sermon" on the first Sunday of the reign, and Cecil took care that there should be no violent outbursts of zeal in public sermons. On the other hand, while Elizabeth was undecided in her policy, it was at once clear that Catholics were to be kept well in hand. When the bishops of Chichester and Winchester[1] preached sermons which were, in the Queen's eyes, injudicious, as outlining the hopes of Catholics, it seemed wisest that they should be at once confined lest they should complicate the diplomacy of the government.

The Bishop of Winchester's sermon, however, contained a prophecy which proved only too true: "At this present time I warn you the wolves be coming out of Geneva and other places of Germany, and have sent their books before, full of pestilent doctrines, blasphemy and heresy to infect the people." The "wolves" soon began to make matters difficult even for the wisest Tudor caution. Interpreting the news which they received from England as favourable to their designs, they began to return from their continental places of exile whither they had fled during Mary's reign. Some of them arrived in England early in December, 1558, and they soon made their presence felt with all the controversial theology of Frankfort, Geneva and Strassburg at their disposal. Their brethren who as yet did not return to England soon "sent

[1] *Zurich Letters*, I. iv. Strype, *Ecclesiastical Memorials*, III. ii. No. lxxxi. (Oxford, 1822). The bishop of Chichester's imprisonment is doubtful (cf. *Vatican MSS.* 64. t. 28. f. 260.) and depends on the *Zurich Letters*.

their books," and the country began to be well
supplied with patronizing and unsolicited literature. Riot and debate followed, and the government enforced silence, allowing the Epistle and
Gospel however to be read in English, but without
comment. These exiles did much in the future, as
we shall see, to disturb the peace of parochial life.

The government at this point apparently asked
for suggestions as to how they should proceed—
and three schemes survive.[1] Among these suggestions several appear which are worthy of consideration. All temporal lands and stately houses
should be taken from the Bishops, and the wealth
from these sources given to needy noblemen.
Alterations in religion must proceed slowly
" having respect to quiet at home, the affairs you
have in hand with foreign princes, the greatness
of the Pope, and how dangerous it is to make
alterations in religion specially in the beginning
of a prince's reign." Care must be taken lest the
" Bishop of Rome be incensed " and proceed to
excommunication, and changes will anger " men
which be of the papist sect . . . . . who will join
and conspire with the bishops and clergy." At
any rate if the alteration is not complete and if any
compromise is made, many will call it " a cloaked

---

[1] (a) " Waad's scheme," *State Papers Domestic*, i. 66.
(b) " The Device for the Alteration of Religion," *Cotton
MSS*. (Brit. Mus.) Julius. F. vi. f, 161, (printed from
this source in Strype, *Annals*, I. ii. No. iv.). Another
manuscript copy is among the *Yelverton MSS*. (Vol.
xxxix. f. 141), printed from this source in Pocock's
Burnet, v. p. 497).
(c) " The Divers Points of Religion contrary to the
Church of Rome," *State Papers Domestic*, i. 68. (cf.
Dixon, *Church History*, v. 28).

papistry or a mingle mangle." In foreign countries, such as Scotland and France, let the government encourage religious factions, but nothing is to be feared from Rome " but evil will, cursing and practising." The bishops and clergy must be forced to accept any changes by penal laws, and *praemunire* should be held out as a threat. Let all irregular innovations in worship, from whatever source, be abolished, only let there be communion in both kinds and Mass seldomer than previously, without any elevation of the Host and always with communicants. Married clergy can be winked at. The prominent Catholic prelates should be committed to the Tower and the rest commanded to keep their houses. When the new Prayer Book comes out let it be accompanied by " straight laws " in order that excessive reformation may be nipped in the bud. No suggestions survive from any Catholic source, and it is more than probable that such were not asked for. Those to which reference has been made bore fruit almost immediately. Thus a characteristic " proceeding warily " marked the earlier relations with the Roman Court. The English agent there, Sir Edward Carne, continued in office, but he was forbidden to see the Pope, excusing himself on the plea that an important ambassador was on his way. There can be no doubt that the relations of Elizabeth with Paul IV were inspired by the tactful suggestions of these papers. That Paul IV took up a corresponding attitude of forbearance is established by the chain of historical evidence which conclusively proves that Paul IV never pronounced

Elizabeth illegitimate, never publicly attacked
her for schism, and that she was never moved in
the direction of Protestant reform by Paul IV's
insults or threats—statements which are commonly
received as history.[1] The Royal Chapel at Christmas also bore witness to the influence of these suggestions. It is believed that the celebrating
bishop on Christmas Day refused to omit the elevation and that the Queen left the chapel.[2] The
defect was remedied on the following days. Thus
the earlier weeks of the reign were characterized
by a slow and tentative policy. As yet the Catholic
bishops took no concerted action. They hoped that
the diplomatic action with regard to Rome spoke
well for the Church, and, in addition, procedure
had not passed very widely beyond the secrecy of
the Council Chamber. The Spanish ambassador,
however, saw in this secrecy no cause for hope, and
reported to his government that three new members
of the Council governed the kingdom; he had
hopes, however, that Dr. Wotton, the Catholic Dean
of Canterbury, would be made Archbishop. Such
a hope was outside the sphere of possibility. The
Queen, Cecil, and Bacon, confirmed the vague reports of the Reforming party by calling to the see
of Canterbury Matthew Parker[3]—a married priest,
who at Mary's accession was deprived on account
of being married[4] and had lived in obscurity

[1] Maitland, *op. cit.*, p. 165.
[2] *Ibid*, p. 170 (cf. *Spanish Calendar* 1. 17 and *Venetian
Calendar* vii. 2). Another account says that the Queen
left after the Gospel. Ellis, *Original Letters* (2nd series),
ii. p. 262 (1827).
[3] *Parker Correspondence*, xl-xlvi.; li.
[4] *Additional MSS.* (Brit. Mus.) 5828, f. 6. *Lansdowne
MSS.* (Brit. Mus.) 981, f. 119.

through her reign. Parker was a man of high aims and a scholar of enthusiastic zeal, who would have preferred the life of a university don to that of a bishop. He was admirably suited to the work to which he was called, not so much by any outstanding originality, as by the fact that his religious opinions fitted in with the developing proposals of the government. He had held many preferments under Edward VI, and his adherence to the Reformation was strong and clear-marked. Indeed it may be said that Parker was by far the most conscientious man in ecclesiastical life during Elizabeth's reign, and he lent a colour to the Established Church which has never been obscured.

Thus then the opening months of the year brought about no changes in parochial life. In the inner circles of authority, however, movements were on foot which were the preludes of change. In these early weeks, as we have seen, plans were matured which were destined to affect the life of the nation in a surprising degree. Before Parliament met, Elizabeth and her advisers knew their line of action, and the transformation of parish life in Elizabethan England owes its inception to the early diplomacy which has been traced in this chapter.

CHAPTER II.

THE FOUNDATIONS OF CHANGE.

QUEEN ELIZABETH was crowned in Westminster Abbey on January 15th, 1559—the last coronation in English history with the Catholic rite and ceremonies. It is no exaggeration to say that many eyes in Europe were turned to Westminster Abbey that day. Rome, Spain, France, Scotland, Geneva, Frankfort waited for the event, as well as the rank and file of Englishmen, for it was clear that the Queen's coronation would give the first public hint of her religious policy. Catholics and Reformers alike looked forward to the event with more than ordinary interest, hoping to find in it some hopes for their respective positions. The records of the Coronation are unfortunately confusing. It is clear, however, that the Queen was determined to demand some changes in the service, and this doubtless influenced Archbishop Heath of York and several of his brethren in their refusal to take part in the ceremony, though they were present in Westminster Abbey. It is impossible to decide what the actual changes were. I am disposed to believe that the Elevation was omitted and that the Queen did not communicate, that the celebrant was Dr. George Carew, a man who had conformed under Edward VI and Mary, and that the actual coronation was performed by Oglethorpe, Bishop of Carlisle.[1] At any rate there were some signi-

---

[1] For a discussion of Elizabeth's Coronation, see *English Historical Review*, xxii. pp. 650 ff.; xxiii. pp. 87 ff.

ficant changes, and Catholics interpreted them as forerunners of further reformation, while the Reformers saw in the general Catholicity of the service an indication that there would be an attempt to prevent the new régime from advancing to the extreme position hoped for in the concluding years of Edward VI.

Parliament opened on January 25th, 1559, and the legislation of the session affected the entire parochial life of the country. With regard to the *personnel* of the House of Lords, the spiritual peers had been reduced, as we have seen, by death. In the House of Commons,[1] it seems that one-third of the members of Mary's last parliament were re-elected, and there can be little doubt that their re-election reflected the reaction in national feeling produced by the Spanish match. The writs summoning Parliament, however, contained a characteristic piece of Tudor astuteness. Cecil deliberately inserted in them a non-committal " &c." Elizabeth was " Queen of England, France and Ireland," and " &c." as well, which Maitland interprets, " &c.—and (if future events shall so decide but not further or otherwise) of the Church of England and also of Ireland upon earth the Supreme Head."[2] There can hardly be found in these early days of Elizabethan statecraft a more valuable example of shrewdness. To Catholics the omission of " Supreme Head " still lent hope; to Reformers who might scruple at the omission, " &c." could

---

[1] *Ibid.*, xxiii. pp. 455 ff., 643 ff.
[2] See Maitland, *op. cit.*, p. 165; and for Cecil's deliberation in the matter of " &c.," see *State Papers Domestic*, i. 3.

be explained as covering everything which they
could desire with regard to the Queen's relationship to the Church. The opening of Parliament
however at once showed the direction which events
were likely to take. The Queen commanded the
Monks of Westminster to take away the torches
which they carried in procession, and Dr. Cox, a
married priest, preached a violent sermon against
monks, images, and Catholic ceremonial.[1] The
actual legislation was preceded by ambiguous de-
bates, and there still remains much doubt about
dates, divisions and procedure.[2] Bacon, the Lord
Keeper, without doubt well acquainted with what
the policy aimed at, in his speech covering
general considerations for the coming discussions,
advised moderation in speech,[3] the avoidance of
such names as " heretic," " schismatic " and
" papist." Before coming to the two important
measures—the Acts of Supremacy and Uniformity
—we may notice that tenths and first fruits were
once again given to the Crown, that the religious
houses which the piety of Mary's reign had founded
were dissolved, and that Elizabeth was declared
Queen of England without any Act annulling her
attainder, or the divorce of her mother, Anne
Boleyn.[4] These matters were insignificant in the
eyes of Catholics, who knew that the real issue lay

[1] See *Venetian Calendar*, 22. (30 Jan. 1559), and compare *Collection des Chroniques Belges inédites*, CCXCV,
i. 413.
[2] For the most careful and scholarly account, see Professor Pollard's volume in *The Political History of England*
(v. pp. 200 ff.).
[3] D'Ewes, *Journal of Parliament*, 14.
I. Eliz., cps. iii., iv., xxiv.

in the attitude adopted by Parliament to the Pope
and to Catholic faith, worship and practice; and
as they expected, these were duly dealt with. Discussions on a Supremacy Bill in Parliament at once
seem to have had effect on the Canterbury House
of Convocation, of which Bonner, Bishop of
London, acted as president, the primacy being
vacant. The Lower House passed a series of
articles[1] which were a strong protest on behalf
of Catholicism. They were five in number:

1 : That in the Sacrament of the Altar, by
    virtue of the words of Christ, duly spoken
    by the priest, is present *realiter*, under the
    kinds of bread and wine, the natural body
    of Christ, conceived of the Virgin Mary, and
    also his natural blood.

2 : That after the consecration there remains
    not the substance of bread and wine, nor
    any other substance but the substance of
    God and man.

3 : That in the Mass is offered the true body
    of Christ and his true blood, a propitiatory
    sacrifice for the living and the dead.

4 : That to Peter the Apostle, and his lawful
    successors, as Christ's vicars, is given the
    supreme power of feeding and ruling the
    Church of Christ militant and confirming
    their brethren.

5 : That the authority of handling and defining
    concerning the things belonging to faith,
    sacraments and discipline ecclesiastical hath
    hitherto ever belonged, and ought to belong

[1] Strype, *Annals*, I., i. 81.

only to the pastors of the Church, whom
the Holy Ghost for this purpose hath set
in the Church, and not to laymen.

The Universities had strengthened the hands of
Convocation by agreeing to the first four articles,
and the five were presented to the Upper House of
Convocation on February 28, 1559, and passed
with a request that they should be laid before the
House of Lords as a petition. Bishop Bonner reported to Convocation that he had presented the
petition in due course to Bacon the Lord Keeper.
In connexion with these articles it is important to
notice that they were passed when the question of
the Royal Supremacy was under discussion in Parliament, that they show in concise form that the
bishops and clergy adhered to the teaching of the
Catholic Church on subjects which were chiefly in
dispute between the Church and the Reformers,
and that they were passed by a body on which
the Government of the day brought no pressure
to bear with regard to election and matter for
debate.[1] We shall see later what answer this petition received. It was in its final analysis an answer
by " laymen."

When the debate on Supremacy was resumed
in March in the House of Lords, the Catholic
Bishops presented a solid front. Archbishop
Heath in a speech[2] of studied moderation upheld

[1] See Father Pollen in *The Dublin Review* (January,
1903), "Many, alas! very many of the clergy subsequently
conformed when sufficient pressure had been brought to
bear upon them; but this, far from impairing the value of
their testimony given under difficulties while they were still
free, on the contrary rather enhances it."

[2] *Corpus Christi, Cambridge MSS.*, cxxi. 20 (Strype,
Annals, I., ii. pp. 399 ff.).

the Catholic position.   He maintained that the Queen was " by the appointment of God indeed sovereign lord and lady, our emperor and empress" in all temporal matters, but to concede that she was " Supreme Head of the Church of England immediate and next under God " meant, "first, that we must forsake and flee from all general councils; secondly, we must flee from all canonical and ecclesiastical laws of the Church of Christ; third, from the judgment of all other Christian princes; fourth and last, we must forsake and flee from the unity of Christ's Church, and by leaping out of Peter's ship, hazard ourselves to be overwhelmed and drowned in the waters of schism, sects, and divisions."   On the third reading on March 18th, Bishop Scot[1] of Chester defended the unity of the Church under Peter and his successors, and appealed to the fact that " at the present there be abroad in Christendom thirty-four sundry sects of opinions, whereof never one agreeth with another, and all differ from the Catholic Church," and all " alledging Scripture " for their doctrines.   The Bill was " with great difficulty forced through all its stages before Easter."[2]   The Queen however refused her consent, acting under the influence of the Spanish Ambassador.   The Supremacy Bill revived the Edwardine statute providing for Communion in both kinds.   The Queen's refusal to sign it before Easter Sunday, March 26, raised the question of the manner of giving the Easter Communion throughout England.   A Royal Pro-

[1] Strype, *op. cit.*, pp. 408 ff.
[2] Maitland, *op. cit.*, p. 199.

clamation[1] was issued on March 22nd which provided for the emergency by stating that the statute
of Edward VI was in force, and that the people
should receive their Easter Communion under both
kinds. Consideration was also taken of the fact
that some of the clergy might not carry out this
proclamation, and might refuse to give Communion
as ordered to their people. The people are advised
not to disturb or molest such clergy, and to pay
their dues to them. They can seek Communion
from others who will carry out the Royal wishes.
In the Royal Chapel the Edwardine rite was
followed on Easter day, and Communion was given
in both kinds, the celebrant wearing only a surplice.[2] The bold front presented by the clergy in
Convocation and by the bishops in the House of
Lords showed the Queen that she must once
more fall back on diplomacy if the question of
Supremacy was to be settled. She determined not
to precipitate her policy by taking the title,
" Supreme Head." She wished to know how far
she could carry the people with her in case of any
popular propaganda on behalf of Catholicism. She
had waited long for power, and she was ready to
make any effort to prevent it slipping from her now
that she had obtained it. It was evident that the
Reforming party in the House of Lords were not
conspicuous in debate where, according to Jewel,
" the bishops ruled as sole monarchs and easily
overreached our little party."[3] The situation was

[1] Dyson, *Proclamations*, f. 5.
[2] *Venetian Calendar*, 57.
[3] *Zurich Letters*, i. p. 9.

C

becoming serious, and an arrangement was made
by which the champions of the Church were to be
discredited in public. A public debate was decided
on between selected Catholics and Reformers.
There can be little doubt that the whole business
was a prearranged plan to educate public opinion
in the changes contemplated.[1]   The articles for
debate are noteworthy: that public prayers and
sacraments should be in a language understood by
the people; that a provincial church without the
bidding of a general council may change rites and
ceremonies, and that the Mass was not a propitiatory sacrifice.[2]   It is significant that the first and
second articles dealt with questions under discussion in Parliament, and that the third contradicted
the unanimous verdict of Convocation already referred to.   The details of this famous disputation,
which began on March 31, 1559, are still in
question; but I think that the Catholic champions
did not follow a proper course, and Archbishop
Heath and Abbot Feckenham of Westminster pro-
tested against their procedure.   On the other hand
the Spanish Ambassador stated[3] that the Blessed
Sacrament had been publicly insulted, and that
the Catholic disputants could not in conscience
continue the debate.   Whatever may be the details
concerned with the actual debate,[4] the government

[1] Strype, *op. cit.*, I. i. p. 137.
[2] *Zurich Letters*, i. p. 10.
[3] *Chroniques Belges*, cccxxxiii. 489.
[4] See Pocock, *Burnet*, v. pp. 507 ff.   The printed
official account is also in Burnet from a copy among the
Corpus Christi, Camb. MSS. (cxxi. 21).   There are three
copies in the *State Papers Domestic*, III., one of which
is corrected by Cecil.   Compare Jewel, *Works* I., pp.
59 ff., and *Zurich Letters* i., p. 27.

succeeded in lowering the Catholic cause in the eyes of the public. The conference broke up with the words of the President, Sir Nicholas Bacon, " For that you will not that we should hear you, you may perhaps shortly hear of us." Immediate disaster followed. Two of the Catholic debaters —Bishops Watson and White—were sent to the Tower, and thus two votes were lost to the Catholic party in the House of Lords, and their companions were heavily fined, confined to a definite area, and obliged to make the Council daily acquainted with their abode and doings.

When Parliament resumed its sittings on April 3rd, a new Supremacy Bill was introduced and passed against the united vote of the Catholic bishops. This is the Elizabethan Act of Supremacy.[1] The anti-papal legislation of Henry VIII was revived. The spiritual jurisdiction of any foreign prelate in England was abolished. The rights of spiritual and ecclesiastical jurisdiction and visitation were annexed to the Crown, with the power to reform and redress heresies and errors. All clergy and all persons holding authority under the Crown were required to take the " Oath of Supremacy "—that the Queen was " the only supreme governor of this realm . . . in all spiritual and ecclesiastical things "—under penalty of deprivation. The maintaining of the power and jurisdiction of any foreign prelate in England by any means whatever was punishable by severe penalties, and if persisted in, by death. Finally, permission was granted to the Crown to

[1] I. Eliz., c. I.

appoint Commissioners to carry out the Supreme
Governorship, and nothing was to be considered
as heresy which did not contradict Scripture, the
first four general councils, the decrees of any other
council based on Scripture, or anything else that
Parliament and Convocation should declare to be
heresy.   The die was cast.   The Parliament of
" laymen " cast out the Pope from England, the
Queen became Supreme Governor of the Church,
which was only another name for Supreme Head;
—Elizabeth "was undisputed sovereign over Church
and   State   alike "[1];   all   ecclesiastical   jurisdiction flowed out from the Crown, and in future
the parochial clergy must take an oath acknow-
ledging the new régime.   This then is the first
great foundation of change in the parochial life
of the reign.   The second followed immediately.
The details with regard to the abolition of Catholic
worship and the provision of a Protestant Prayer
book must be read elsewhere.   The final scenes
connected   with   the   Act   of   Uniformity   were
dramatic.   Bishop Thirlby boldly declared that he
would rather die than be a party to a change of
religion.   Bishop Scot rose to a lofty height of
pathetic eloquence in his appeal for the rejection
of the Bill.   Nine spiritual and nine temporal
peers voted against it; twenty-one temporal peers
voted in its favour.   Four spiritual peers were absent.   The Act,[2] which came into force on June
24th, was penal.   All spiritual persons refusing to
use the new service book—the Second Prayer Book

[1] Pollard, *op. cit.*, p. 215.
[2] I. Eliz., c. ii.

of Edward VI with slight modifications—were liable to fines, deprivation or imprisonment, the last for life in case of a third conviction. Equally severe penalties were enacted against words or writings derogatory to the book. Absence from the new services on Sundays and Holydays was punished by a fine of twelve pence for each offence. This fine was to be collected by the church-wardens, while the Bishops and other Ordinaries were at the same time to administer ecclesiastical censures. Finally, a section specially provided that the old ornaments of the church and ministers should remain in use as in the first year of Edward VI, until the Queen saw fit to make a change by the advice of a body of Commissioners or of the Primate. This section is important in connexion with many parochial disputes of the future. Thus, as under Edward VI, the Mass and Catholic worship were driven from England under the severest penalties. No other form of public service " openly or privately " was allowed. This Act is the second great foundation of parochial change, and its influence is incalculable. Not merely was Catholic worship a penal offence, but the people were deprived of the moral support which they most needed at the time, and compelled to resort to Protestant worship. We shall see in detail how parochial life became a dreary round of inquiry and inquisition through these regulations. It is well to remember that the New Prayer Book lacked any approval by the Church. It was part of an Act of Parliament and enforced by an Act of Parliament, against which every spiritual peer present

in the House of Lords had voted. The issue will
show a large conformity by the people as the years
go on, but it must never be forgotten that they had
in reality no say in the erection of a new religion,
and in depriving themselves of their natural bul-
warks against religious change. The forces of
change broke round them when they were cut adrift
from the practices and support of their religion.
London did not wait for midsummer. The New
Service Book was at once ushered into all the parish
churches there amid scenes of sacrilege and icono-
clasm.

With the new machinery ready, no time was lost
in starting it to work. A Royal Commission was
issued by the Council on May 23, 1559, and this
commission was entrusted with tendering the Oath
of Supremacy to the clergy.[1] Its members were
all known to be in sympathy with the Reformation.
They immediately began to work by tendering
the Oath to the Catholic Bishops, who had fought
so valiantly for the Church since the beginning of
the reign. Before the end of the year all were
deprived except two. The story of their fortitude
and their sufferings has been frequently told, and
must be read elsewhere.[2] Their deprivation at
once left the dioceses of England desolate of
Catholic authority, and cut them off from the unity
of the Church. In this desolation and isolation
all the parishes in the land shared. The with-
drawal of Catholic diocesan government was but

[1] Rymer, *Foedera*, xv. p. 518.
[2] Father Phillips, *op. cit.*, and Bridgett and Knox,
Queen Elizabeth and The Catholic Hierarchy (1889).

the prelude to parochial disintegration. The monks and nuns of the Marian religious houses were soon driven into exile, and plans were at once matured for a Royal Visitation, under the Act of Supremacy, of the whole kingdom. By June 13th, Cecil had ready a body of fifty-six Royal Articles of Enquiry and of fifty-three Royal Injunctions, to which was appended a liberal interpretation of the " Oath of Supremacy,"[1] the outcome of considerable opposition to it in the country. The entire kingdom was divided up among lay and clerical visitors acting for the Crown, and arrangements seem to have been completed by July, 1559, for the momentous work of changing the parochial life of England. The ordinary ecclesiastical administration, as might be expected, was completely suspended, and the visitors acted as ecclesiastical judges, and were authorized to enforce the " settlement of religion," as outlined in the Acts of Supremacy and Uniformity and in the Royal Injunctions. We have already considered the two statutes as foundations of parochial change. It is now necessary to analyze the Royal Injunctions, as this body of royal orders formed the basis of parochial government for almost the entire reign. It is of course outside the scope of our survey to consider the result of this Royal Visitation in relation to the clergy. All that need be said here is that only a small percentage of them remained true to the Catholic Faith, but recent research goes to show that this percentage must be placed higher

[1] For the Royal Articles and Injunctions, see Dr. Gee, *The Elizabethan Clergy*, pp. 46 ff.

than that usually given by Protestant historians.

Careful attention is needed to the Royal Injunctions, as they provide the broad outlines for the parochial picture which we shall attempt, in the ensuing chapters, to fill in in detail.   It is necessary to remember that their application to parochial life was almost continuous, and the clergy were compelled to bring them regularly before their parishioners, and to enforce them in their parishes.   A detailed analysis of them at this point will not only facilitate the study of parochial life, but it is emphatically necessary at the beginning of the study.   Through all the fluctuations and changes of the national life during the reign, they held their place.   They became part and parcel of the very fibres of diocesan administration, and of local life in every parish in England.

The clergy were ordered to preach at least four times every year that the Pope's power in England was justly abolished, and that the Queen was Supreme Governor of the Church.   In addition, they were to warn their parishioners that pilgrimages, candles, praying upon beads, were superstitions under the curse of God as idolatry.   A sermon or a prescribed Homily must be read every Sunday, and regular teaching on the Lord's Prayer, Creed and Ten Commandments in English must be given every holyday.   They must provide an English Bible in the church, with the Paraphrases of Erasmus, and no one must be hindered from reading the same.   They must avoid alehouses and taverns, and give themselves to godly living and the study of the Scriptures.   They must present

to the justices of the peace any of their parishioners who may interrupt or hinder the new services,
or favour the Pope's religion. They must keep a
parochial register for baptisms, weddings and
burials. If they are not resident in their parishes,
they must distribute a fortieth part of their income
among the poor. They must maintain scholars at
the Universities, and keep their residences in
thorough repair. They must read the Injunctions
in church publicly every quarter. They must prepare certain books of the Scripture for examination
during visitations, learning portions of them in
order to comfort the sick and afflicted. They must
wear decent, seemly habits as becomes their office.
Their preaching and reading must be plain and
distinct in order to encourage godliness. If they
wish to marry, they must bring the ladies of their
choice to the diocesan bishop and two justices of
the peace for approval.[1] All processions in the
church were forbidden, but the parish could be
" perambulated " on the Rogation Days without
ceremonies. All ringing of bells must cease except one bell before the sermon. Permission was
granted to the people for harvesting on holydays
after attendance at Common Prayer. All " shrines,
pictures, paintings and other monuments of feigned
miracles, pilgrimages, idolatry and superstition, so
that there remain no memory of the same in walls,
glass windows and elsewhere within the churches
and houses," must be utterly destroyed, and no one

---

[1] For examples of such licenses to the clergy to marry,
Parker MS. Register, i. 205, 298, and *Loseley MSS.*,
p. 254. For the Queen's contempt for clerical marriage
see *Parker Correspondence*, pp. 148, 157.

may henceforth keep any such objects of piety in
their homes. A " comely and decent " pulpit must
be provided in every church with a poor-box in
which the people are to place the money which
they once spent " on pardons, pilgrimages, trentals,
decking of images, offering of candles, giving to
friars and other like blind devotions." All parochial monies originally bequeathed for requiems
must be given in future to the poor or to the repair
of the churches. The people must respect their
clergy. All heresies must be diligently suppressed.
No one must be absent from Common Prayer, otherwise the fines will be imposed. All alehouses and
taverns must be closed during the times of service
and preaching. Schoolmasters must be examined
and approved in intellectual abilities and Reformation orthodoxy by the Ordinaries. Records must
be kept of those imprisoned, or put to death for religion. Inventories must be drawn up of all the
church ornaments, plate and books, especially those
connected with Catholic worship. Singing in a
" modest and distinct song " may be allowed in
church, while a hymn with music may at times
" comfort those who delight in music." No books
must be printed except those specially licensed by
the Queen, or a committee of the Privy Council,
or Bishops. Due reverence, " with lowliness of
courtesy and uncovering of the head of menkind,"
must be given at the mention of the Holy Name.
All altars must be taken down under the oversight of the clergy and churchwardens, and holy
tables must be decently made and set up where the
altars stood, care being taken that they could be

removed anywhere in the chancels during the Communion Service. Plain white flour bread without any figures on it and thicker than that used for Mass must be used for Communion. " All which and similar instructions, the Queen's Majesty ministereth unto her clergy and to all other her loving subjects, straightly charging and commanding them to observe and keep the same upon pain of deprivation, sequestration of fruits and benefices, suspension, excommunication and such other coercion, as to Ordinaries, or others having ecclesiastical jurisdiction, whom her Majesty hath appointed or shall appoint for the due execution of the same, shall be convenient; charging and commanding them to see these Injunctions observed and kept by all persons under their jurisdiction, as they will answer to her Majesty for the contrary. And her Highness's pleasure is, that every justice of the peace being required, shall assist the Ordinaries, and every one of them, for the due execution of the said Injunctions."

This formidable series of royal orders forms the third foundation of parochial change. It is at once evident that it contained little hope for Catholics. Its most conservative items were soon twisted to Reforming ends, and the wildest zeal was soon let loose in the parishes of England, urged on by the new bishops and clergy. This general scheme for parochial life was enforced everywhere. When the Royal Visitation was suspended, its work was continued by a permanent body known as the Court of High Commission, which for upwards of a century excited the odium of even the most loyal

ceived it, and done it as often as not in spite of
Queen and Government.   His brethren, however,
were men of another stamp   Their individual
characteristics do not concern us, but there are certain features common to them which require to be
noted.   First of all, they were almost entirely
Marian exiles who had returned to England with
all their original reforming zeal fanned into fiery
heat.   Nearly every conceivable degree of Continental Protestantism was represented among them,
from the nebulosity of Zwingli to the mazes of
Luther.   Secondly, they were uncompromising in
their demand for reform.   Before long Parker
found that he had to deal with a body of men
not entirely in sympathy with his own ideals, and
in a degree dissatisfied with the Elizabethan Settlement. Many of them in the future disregarded the
clearest orders of the Prayer Book and Injunctions,
and their parishes reflected their caprice. Many of
them encouraged the extreme Puritan party, wrote
and   preached   against   anything   approaching
Catholicism which was left by Queen and Parliament, and gladly encouraged their clergy to aban-
don   even   the   smallest   decencies   in   worship.
Thirdly, Parker perhaps alone excepted, they were
actuated in all their dealings by the love of money,
and inspired in their outlook by material considerations.   Not a few of them neglected the burden
of diocesan rule, while they sought personal ease.
Finally, from Parker down, they recognized that
they held office from the Government.   No one
can turn over their correspondence without being
convinced of this fact.   If some of them wished

to enforce discipline, a letter to " Mr. Secretary, Cecil " witnessed to the fact that they recognized the source of their authority. If some of them desired further reform, the extreme Puritan nobility carried their desires and laid them as petitions before the same sinister authority. Even Parker, whom the Queen and Cecil most trusted, was taught that his authority was derived from the Crown, and Grindal learned a salutary lesson in the same connexion. In addition, the whole body presented to the nation no united front on doctrine, discipline, ritual, or ceremonial. Their strongest unifying principle was an uncompromising hatred of Catholicism, and in this they were at least consistent, for they themselves rose out of its destruction. The banishment of the Pope from England, and the establishment of a Protestant form of worship constituted their *raison d'être*. It will not be surprising then that the parochial clergy fell far short of those praiseworthy ideals which Parker had for them. We shall see that they were as colourless, as factious, and as incompetent as their bishops.

In Catholic days the parish priest represented in every parish in the land the unity of his parish with the Catholic Church. He offered the same Holy Sacrifice as was offered in every Catholic parish throughout the world. He preached Catholic doctrine, taught the Catholic Faith, and stood before his people as a point of contact in his sacerdotal life with the Church of the Apostles. He poured the cleansing waters of Baptism over the new-born children, and every one believed in the effects of

the Sacrament. He absolved penitents, and no one
doubted that he did so by virtue of his share in
the Priesthood of Jesus Christ. He stood at the
altar arrayed in priestly vestments, and all his
parishioners were convinced that he offered to God
the propitiatory sacrifice of the Body and Blood
of Christ. He prepared men and women and
children for the last lone journey, and they knew
that his preparation had behind it the divine mind
of the Church. Indeed, the parish priest lent unity
to parish life. In addition, he was a man under
authority. His teaching could not reflect individual caprice. His church services could not
suffer change as he or his parishioners might desire.
He had not one line of dealing with the rich and
another with the poor. The diocesan bishop and
the diocesan synod were always ready to control
and direct him. If he failed in his duty, the churchwardens were not slow to present him to the
Ordinary. Of course, there were incompetent
parish priests, lazy parish priests, evil parish
priests. Types such as these usually attain
notoriety, but we cannot condemn a class by its
black sheep any more than we would condemn a
community on its police-court statistics. Indeed
if we take such records as survive, we shall be
compelled to conclude that, as a body, the parish
priests of Catholic England were worthy men, and
certainly they believed and taught the Catholic
Faith, and carried out the duties of their sacred
office with zeal and conviction, before decay set
in with newer forces and newer ideas.[1]

[1] For an admirable short study on the pre-Reformation
clergy, see Dr. Jessopp, *Before the Great Pillage*,
pp. 73 ff. (1910),

When we turn to the Elizabethan clergy we find that we are moving among another type. There is little conviction, little zeal except in repressing Catholicism, little unity of purpose and little respect for authority, although there was no small display of it. At the very utmost, the Elizabethan parish clergyman did not carry the thoughts of his parishioners beyond Lambeth Palace, and certainly not further than the Parliament House. His very presence emphasized the isolation and insularity—if not the parochialism—of his teaching. He represented to his people not a unity with historic Christianity, but a unity with a new State Church, whose Supreme Governor was the Queen, and whose services were controlled by Act of Parliament. He was as much a state official in popular opinion as were the local justices. He repeated prayers hall-marked with the Royal Arms, he read Homilies sanctioned by the Crown, and if he was licensed to preach, his sermons were inspired by the directions of the Government. I am not concerned with modern views of him—nor can he be judged from modern points of view. The only just method of judging him is to see him with contemporary eyes, and I think I have not done injustice to the picture.

The early years of the reign show a remarkable picture of conformity to the new religion on the part of the clergy. If we take the highest possible figure, it cannot be said that more than a thousand refused to accept the Elizabethan changes. The Eastern, Southern and Midland Counties provided more conformists than those of

D

the North and North-west, and the chapters of
the Cathedrals were more " stubborn in papistry,"
as a contemporary document says, than the parochial clergy.   On the other hand there is evidence
that some of the clergy only conformed, " hoping
for a day," that a few of them said Mass in private
and then went through the Protestant Communion
Service.   In connexion with the question of conformity some references to contemporary documents will help to show the state of affairs.
Cardinal Allen declared in the middle of the reign
that " many priests said Mass secretly and celebrated the heretical offices and Suppers in public."[1]
In Durham diocese Bishop Pilkington complained
that Marian priests still carried on the idolatrous
worship in secret, and in 1577 his successor,
Barnes, boasted that he had driven out " the re-
conciling priests and massers whereof there was
store."[2]   In the diocese of Carlisle, Bishop Best
found that " the priests are imps of Antichrist, for
the most part very ignorant and stubborn, past
measure false and subtle; only fear maketh them
obedient."[3] His successor a few years later wrote
that the popish priests lived in secret, but reconciled
the people to Rome in public, and caused them to
abjure the religion of Christ.[4]   In Lancashire,
" massing priests resorted at their pleasure " to the
houses of " recusants " as late as 1590.[5]   In the

---

[1] *Records of English Catholics*, I. xxiii.
[2] *Lansdowne MSS.*, xxv. 78.
[3] *State Papers Domestic*, xviii. 21 (July 19, 1561).
[4] *Ibid.*, lxxiv. 22 (Oct. 27, 1570).
[5] *Cotton MSS.* (Brit. Mus.) Tit. B. iii. 20,

vast diocese of York many priests reconciled num-
bers to papistry in the years preceding 1577.[1] In
the diocese of Worcester " popish and perverse
priests, which misliking religion, have forsaken the
ministry, yet lived in corners, were kept in gentlemen's houses and were had in great estimation of
the people."[2] In the parishes of Hereford diocese
many who held livings in Queen Mary's days went
about as "mortal and deadly enemies to religion ";
many Masses were said in private houses.[3] Up
and down the Fen parishes many ran about " to
hear Mass in private."[4] Massing priests were
found in Coventry and Lichfield in 1584,[5] and
their presence was also noted in 1575 in the large
diocese of Winchester.[6] The entire province of
Canterbury was diligently searched for them in
1576.[7] These examples have been culled almost
at random from the documents of the period, and
I have confined myself to such as appear to refer,
not to missionary priests from abroad, but to
Marian priests who continued in secret to serve
their people. It will thus be seen that there was
grave necessity on the part of the Government to
urge on the new clergy in the work of reform, and
to advance in Reformation principles if they were
to counteract the work of " secret priests " in their
parishes.

[1] *State Papers Domestic*, cxvii. 23 (Oct. 28, 1577).
[2] The report refers to the year 1564. See *Camden Miscellany*, ix. pp. 1 ff.
[3] *Ibid.*, pp. 11 ff.
[4] *Zurich Letters*, xciv. (Feb. 12, 1572).
[5] *Second Ritual Report*, App. E., p. 428.
[6] *Ibid.*, p. 415.   [7] Cardwell, *Annals*, i. 404.

The question now arises: What were the intellectual attainments of the new clergy? Doubtless there was much learning in various quarters among them, and it would be unfair not to state that not a few of them excelled in learned attempts to defend their position. On the other hand, the uniform record of complaints justifies us in concluding that the vast majority of them were men of small intellectual attainments, and the fact that they were ceaselessly urged to study in certain directions amid the troubles of their parochial life, goes far to prove that the standard of learning was generally low among them. In 1560 the ministry of Durham diocese was " barren and destitute of a sufficiency of worthy men."[1] In 1578 Archbishop Sandys of York blamed the clergy for their inability to instruct the people, and from this arose a deplorable state of morals in the parishes.[2] In 1566 the parishes of South-western Wales were reported for being in great need of reform on account of men who lacked " good doctrine and true knowledge." The bishop begged that such incompetent clergy should not be sent to him.[3] In Northern Wales in the following year, ninety per cent. of the clergy were returned as incapable of teaching God's Word and unable to preach.[4] Indeed the parishes of Wales seem to have suffered much from want of learning. In places, children and laymen held benefices, and the Queen was grieved to find that true religion was hindered be-

---

[1] *State Papers Domestic*, xv. 45.
[2] *Lansdowne MSS.*, xxvii. 12.   [3] *Ibid.*, viii. 75.
[4] *State Papers Domestic*, xliv. 27.

cause many of the clergy were incompetent and
unlearned.[1]   Hereford City was a nursery of
clerical ignorance in 1561.[2] In 1584, in the archdeaconry of Staffordshire, scarcely one clergyman
out of a hundred and fifty was fit to preach.[3] In
London during the years 1560 and 1561, Grindal
held several large ordinations, but many of his
candidates were mere tradesmen.   It is not too
much to add that it was one of the jibes of controversy to scoff at the unlearned clergy drawn
from shops and business employments. Indeed
the Reformers themselves admitted the fact while
deploring the necessity for it.[4] On the other hand
the bishops made heroic efforts to improve clerical
scholarship, and they added to the burden of parish
work regular study, upon which the clergy should
be examined at visitations, either by the bishops
or their archdeacons.   This preparation for ex-
aminations, after being ordained and admitted to
a cure of souls or work in a parish, was enforced
during the whole reign on all the parochial clergy.
A general agreement on this matter was arrived
at among the bishops about the year 1561.[5] They
arranged that their clergy should learn by heart
some portions of the New Testament and repeat
them before the diocesan synod, but this rule was
expanded in future years. The clergy of Norwich
diocese were compelled in 1562 to study daily two
chapters of the New Testament until they had

[1] *Cotton MSS.*, Vit. c. i. 12. 118.
[2] *State Papers Domestic*, xvii. 32.
[3] *Egerton MSS.*, 1693. f. 118.
[4] *E.g.*, see Calfhill, *Works*, 51.
[5] See my *Interpretations of the Bishops*, p. 29.

finished the Epistles, and then to present themselves for a detailed examination before the
bishop.[1] In the parishes of Northern Wales, in
the same year, the subject matter for study was
made more difficult by the inclusion of the Latin
text of the New Testament as well as the English,
and Erasmus' *Paraphrase*.[2] This order was extended to all the parish clergy in the North of
England in 1571.[3] In 1565 the parish clergy
of North-eastern Kent were ordered to prepare the
Epistle to the Romans for their examination,[4] and
the order was renewed in general terms for the same
clergy in 1571.[5] These examples illustrate efforts
at improvement, while at the same time they confirm the broad statement that clerical learning was
of a very low order, considering that the prescribed study did not get much beyond a few
chapters of the New Testament. With the advent
of Whitgift as primate attempts were made at a
general levelling-up. Orders were issued in 1584
that no one was to be ordained except a graduate
of one of the Universities, who was able to give
in Latin an account of his faith. In the following
year the examination was extended for all parochial
clergy by the inclusion of the Old Testament, and
it was to be conducted in Latin. Nor were matters
allowed to remain here. The Queen was dis-
tressed at the admission of " unmeet men into the
ministry," and Whitgift issued orders at her in-

[1] *British Museum*, 5155. aa. 8.
[2] Wilkins, *Concilia*, iv. 228.
[3] *Second Ritual Report*, App. E. pp. 411 ff.
[4] *Rochester MSS.*, vii. f. 98v.   [5] *Ibid.*, f. 118.

stigation that a general inquiry should be held into " the degrees, learning and qualities of all ministers." As the reign drew to a close there is evidence of some improvement, but the bishops continued to ask in their visitations if the clergy were " learned men and able to preach," and these questions would seem to point to the fact that many " dumb dogs," as they were contemptuously called, continued in the parishes of England. Preaching against the Pope and the Catholic faith was the chief object aimed at, and the dearth of preachers, considering this aim, is remarkable.

In turning to consider the state of morality among the clergy, we are forced to judge from evidence which is largely negative. I have eliminated the use of the controversial writings of the reign, as they do not seem to me to be trustworthy evidence unless supported from reliable sources. In addition, no serious work has been done on the proceedings in ecclesiastical cases under Queen Elizabeth, and until this is accomplished the study must remain incomplete. However, the records of diocesan visitations are fairly wide. The usual method in these visitations was to send a set of enquiries to every parish, and when the answers had been examined, to issue diocesan injunctions. These questions and injunctions therefore form invaluable material for a survey of parochial life, and in connexion with clerical morals they provide reliable facts, from which certain general features emerge. It will be best to group the evidence for various counties as it is scattered over different years. This method will render the

survey as complete as possible, and reference to
the dates will provide a concise comparative study.
In the documents clerical failures of all kinds are
usually referred to in groups, and it is unnecessary
to differentiate between them.   In all the parishes
south of a line drawn across England from Chester
to Hull, enquiries were made in 1560 if any of the
parochial clergy were simoniacal, given to filthy
lucre, swearers, fornicators, adulterers, drunkards,
gamblers, slanderers, gossips, and if they visited
any suspect houses for evil purposes; also if they
favoured the Pope and taught corrupt doctrines.[1]
Sixteen years later in the same counties these enquiries were repeated and amplified by asking if
the clergy kept suspected women in their houses,
and resorted to taverns and alehouses.[2]   In 1588
the same clergy were ordered to live sober and
abstemious lives.[3]   In all the counties north of
this line the clergy were forbidden in 1571 to
resort with evil women, to live incontinently, to
drink to excess, and to indulge in gambling at dice
and cards.[4] In 1561 enquiries were made in the
county of Norfolk[5] if any of the parochial clergy
had put away their wives in " time of trouble,"
that is in Mary's reign, if such wives were now
married to other men, and their clerical husbands
wedded to other women.   Were they men of im-
moral life, given to gaming and drink?   These
enquiries were repeated in connexion with the same

[1] *University Library, Cambridge MSS.* Mm. 6. 73 (3).
[2] Cardwell, *Annals,* i. p. 406.
[3] *Earl MSS.* (Univ. Lib. Camb.), f. 46v.
[4] *Second Ritual Report,* App. C., p. 412.
[5] *Brit. Mus.* 5155. aa. 8 (1).

clergy in 1569, when enquiries were also made as to whether they had unlawfully sold any goods belonging to their churches.[1] In the central-north of Kent[2] an inquisition into clerical morals was held along the same lines in 1565, including a question with regard to clerical " favouring of the Popish Religion." In the same district in 1572 there is evidence of simony.[3] In the counties of Derby and Stafford[4] the clergy were ordered in 1567 to give up resorting to alehouses, to keep no suspected woman, and no woman under fifty in their houses, wives, sisters, aunts and kinswomen excepted. In the counties of Worcester and Warwick[5] in 1569 questions covering lewd and wanton clerical life, clerical drunkenness and gaming were administered. In 1571 superstitious doctrines were added to similar questions concerning the clergy of London,[6] and in 1585 a like clerical inquisition was held in the southern parishes of Kent and Surrey.[7] The evidence could be extended from similar sources, but it would supply no closer details. On analyzing such evidence as has been given, it may be divided into two divisions, negative from questions, and positive from prohibitions. It is well known that questions in visitations were largely based on existing conditions, while visitation prohibitions were always the outcome of enquiries. Thus then, both the negative

[1] *Second Ritual Report*, App. E., p. 404.
[2] *Rochester MSS.*, vii. f. 98.
[3] *Ibid.*, f. 128v.
[4] *State Papers Domestic*, xxxvi. 42 and 42.
[5] *Lansdowne MSS.*, xi. 204.
[6] *Brit. Mus.*, 698. h. 20 (10).
[7] Cardwell, *Annals*, ii. 25.

and positive evidence of these documents goes to
show that over a wide area of parishes there was
much to be deplored in the state of clerical morality during the reign. I have confined myself pur-
posely to evidence drawn from Protestant sources.
When foreign reports and the books of Catholic
controversialists are examined, they confirm the
conclusion that among the new parochial clergy
there was a distinct and prominent laxity of life.
It is however impossible to conclude from the
evidence before us to what extent this laxity pre-
vailed, but when we have considered in a later
chapter the state of morality among the laity, and
seen to what a deplorable condition it sank, it can
at least be said that it reflected in no small degree
the clerical shortcomings. In neither case can we
arrive at any definite estimate, but the general tone
of the documents and the repeated questions and
prohibitions over many years in this connexion,
justify us in saying that there were serious moral
shortcomings among a large number of clergy and
people.

Finally, it may be well to sum up under general
terms the ordinary duties of an Elizabethan parish
clergyman. He was required to provide Sunday
services in his parish church, and to use in them
exclusively the Book of Common Prayer. He was
ordered to catechize the children regularly on
Sundays and holydays; to read the Royal Injunctions; to exercise hospitality; to direct the people
in making their wills; to examine those about to
be married in their knowledge of the reformed
faith; to take care that fines for non-attendance

at church were imposed; to keep the registers carefully and to send copies to his Ordinary; to make a list of those who did not come to Communion at Easter; to preach—if able and licensed—regular sermons in favour of the Queen's ecclesiastical supremacy, and against "the Pope's usurped authority, now justly banished"; and generally to carry out the details of the new religious régime.

It would take us too far afield to consider such questions as clerical residence, or the growth of Puritan opinions, and a consequent nonconformity among the clergy. Nor can the question of clerical marriage be discussed. The statistics in this connexion show a varied proportion. For example, in 1562 in the archdeaconry of London, more than half the clergy were married, but only a seventh in that of St. Albans.[1] It would seem at any rate that clerical marriage was sufficiently common to keep the bishops and magistrates busy in examining the chosen ladies according to the Royal Injunctions. It is also interesting to note that at one period the Queen was so dissatisfied with the general progress of the Reformation and the state of religion, that she ordered the cathedral clergy to live apart from their wives, and was with difficulty dissuaded from showing her disgust with the parochial clergy as a body by issuing a general injunction forbidding clerical marriage.[2]

[1] See *Parker MSS.* (Corpus Christi College, Cambridge), xcvii. and cxxii., and *Additional MSS.* (British Museum), 5813.
[2] See *Parker Correspondence*, Nos. cv., cvii., cix., cxiv.

CHAPTER IV.

THE PARISH CHURCH.

A PRE-REFORMATION parish church in England was the pride of every parishioner, not only because it was the Holy of Holies, the centre of his highest aspirations, the house of his sacrifice and prayer, but also because it was the age-long memorial of parochial charity. His ancestors had built it. His friends had furnished it in all the beauty of holiness, and he himself gladly helped to enrich its possessions and to preserve it against time and weather. The pious Catholics in Mary's reign had done much to refit the parish churches of England after the great pillage under Edward VI, and not a few accounts have come down to us of their success in re-beautifying them. It will be well to enter one of these Marian churches in order to gain some idea of them.

The first impression on passing through the porch into the nave must be that there was a general atmosphere of devotion and awe. The stained-glass windows, in whose lights were figured Saints of the Church belonging to every land, cast " a dim religious light." Near the door was a cut-stone font covered with a magnificent canopy of carved pine or oak. The pews or seats —if such existed—were beautiful specimens of woodwork. Here and there round the nave stood statues of the Saints in niches of carved stone. As we stand at the door, what at once strikes us

is the chancel or east end of the church, cut off
from the nave by a magnificent screen of wonderful
and intricate work richly painted and gilt, crowned
by a " broad loft " running from pillar to pillar
of the chancel arch, which was usually reached by
two circular staircases in the pillars.   High above
this loft on the rood-beam stood the cross of tim-
ber, richly carved and coloured, with figures of Our
Lady and St. John.   Coronals of silver or less
valuable metal were suspended on all the great
rood-lofts, and filled with lighted tapers on solemn
feasts.   This screen spoke to the people of the
dignity of the Holy Sacrifice of the Mass, the
highest act of the Catholic religion; and it stood
as a permanent witness of Catholic tradition, that
the place of Sacrifice should be railed off from the
rest of the church.   The Mass is a great *act*, something to be done, not heard or seen.   Inside the
chancel stood the high altar, practically furnished
as we know it to-day.   A suspended light burned
before the Blessed Sacrament, reserved since the
time of Cardinal Pole in a tabernacle on the altar,
and not suspended in a hanging pyx, as had been
the old English custom.[1]   The church was provided with all 'the necessaries of worship—vestments, bells, candles, thuribles, processional
crosses, complete sets of service books and of altar
vessels.   Not a few of these had been preserved
through the vandalism of the reign of Edward VI,
being hidden by the people in hope of a better

[1] See *Harleian MSS.* (Brit. Mus.), cccxci. f. 4. Compare Reynolds' *Constitutions* (1322); *Bonner MS. Register*,
f. 365 (47) and Wriothesley, *Chronicle*, ii., 114.

day; but the vast majority of them had been bought and provided during Mary's reign, to supply the places of those destroyed in times of persecution and Catholic repression.

From the beginning of Queen Elizabeth's reign a controversy arose over Church ornaments. We have seen that the Act of Uniformity provided for the use of old vestments, and that the Royal Injunctions ordered inventories of them to be drawn up, together with church plate and books. We have also seen that the royal orders in the general visitation included a peremptory command to destroy images and paintings, whether in the walls or windows. The controversy arose out of the fact that the Injunctions provided for the destruction of altars, and placed vestments, books, and church plate in such a connexion as to make it doubtful whether the government meant them to be preserved. The drawing-up of inventories under Edward VI prefaced the destruction of church goods, and the Elizabethan dealings show that they were destroyed with " other monuments of superstition," if the parsons and churchwardens considered them as such. The whole history of legality or illegality lies beyond our survey, and it will be sufficient to review in some detail the changes which completely remodelled the parish churches of England.

As early as the middle of August, 1559, the Spanish Ambassador[1] noticed that all the altars, crosses and images had been removed from the London churches. A few days later Machyn,[2] the

[1] *Spanish Calendar* (13 Aug. 1559).
[2] *Diary,* pp. 207 ff.

contemporary diarist, noted a singular *auto da fé*
in London, when crosses, images, censers, altar
cloths, books and banners were burned " with great
wonder." At this period similar scenes were
enacted all over the parishes of England. Bishop
Tunstall, the last Catholic bishop of Durham, complained that many churches of his vast diocese
were denuded of their ornaments, and the valuable
churchwardens' accounts for the year 1559 contain
detailed records of the burning or sale of " papistical books, idols and pictures, banners, chrisma-
tories, paxes, bells, pyxes, vestments, roods and all
other idols." In a few cases isolated items of
Church goods survived, but as a general rule everything connected with Catholic worship was destroyed. In not a few instances the vestments were
made into dresses for the wives of the clergymen
or uniforms for soldiers, or served as covers for
fonts, pulpits or Communion tables. Most important perhaps of all, the altars were removed, often
amid scenes of revolting profanity. They had
served their day with the abolition of the Holy
Sacrifice. Nor was the sacredness of the homes of
the people respected. Search was made in them
for any images and for holy pictures, and these
were ruthlessly destroyed with the church ornaments. The dealings of the Visitors turned the
parishes of England into wholesale areas of wanton
destruction. Every shrine and picture, every
tabernacle and altar, every image and relic of the
Saints was handed over to brutal sacrilege. The
fate of chalices and patens has an interesting history. The paten is rarely mentioned, but it seems

clear that there was some general order given forbidding the use of the old chalices, which is not now forthcoming. In some places they escaped, but as early as 1559 we find that they were sold, and from 1565 we find that the records of these sales become more detailed. On the other hand I am inclined to believe that from the very beginning the government meant them to be destroyed, as a record[1] for 1560 tells us that a clergyman was reported for having and using a " popish chalice." From 1565 onwards regular orders were issued to the clergy to use, instead of these chalices, decent cups of silver, and this order was frequently accompanied by another commanding them to do away with their " superstitious chalices."[2] However, the parsimony of the age in connexion with religion soon invented something more practical than destruction. A general order[3] seems to have been issued before the year 1569 ordering the clergy to turn their chalices into " decent communion cups." This order is however not forthcoming, but there was a motion passed in Convocation in 1563 that " chalices be altered to decent cups."[4]

In the Royal Chapel the Queen for a time played with the use of a cross or crucifix (these names are almost always used as convertible terms), but crosses and crucifixes seem early to have shared the common destruction " as idolatrous images."

---

[1] *Archdeacons' MSS.* (Canterbury, 1560).

[2] *E.g.*, see *Rochester MSS.*,vii., f. 98., *Norwich Articles* (Brit. Mus.), T. 1015 (1).

[3] *State Papers Domestic*, lx. 71.

[4] Strype, *Annals*, I. ii., App. A.

They were destroyed in the parishes of London in 1559, and this noteworthy example of the capital seems to have inspired zeal throughout the provincial parishes. We have valuable manuscript returns for Lincolnshire extending over the years 1559—1566. Only nine crosses stood in churches in the latter year, and this in a country thickly studded with churches. In a few instances we have records of their being sold, but as a general rule they were demolished. The manuscript evidence extant goes to prove how bitterly the Reformers hated the sign of our Redemption. Thus, for example,[1] it was destroyed in central England in 1569 as a " monument of gross superstition and idolatry." In 1571 a searching enquiry was made in all the northern counties,[2] and " every cross " remaining in any church was singled out to be " utterly defaced, broken, and destroyed." Even the stone crosses in graveyards were destroyed in Hampshire in the same year.[3] The records of the wholesale destruction of objects of Catholic piety are pitifully plentiful. It would be possible to take every class of church ornament and to write a long chapter on its history, so wide are the documents at our disposal. We can, however, only select one further subject for consideration—the fate of the Catholic service books. Under Queen Mary pious Catholics carried out Cardinal Pole's order[4] for their re-provision in the churches after the Edwardine pillage. When Elizabeth restored

[1] *Lansdowne MSS.*, xi. f. 204.
[2] *Second Ritual Report*, App. E., p. 411.
[3] *Horne MS. Register*, f. 81v.
[4] *Pole MS. Register*, f. 34.

E

the Protestant service, orders were issued to draw
up a list of old service books. This order was
interpreted in the light of previous dealings, and
as a general rule they shared the early fate of
" monuments of gross superstition and blasphemous
idolatry." A few have found a place among the
treasures of the nation, or of private individuals.
But the work was not confined to these earlier
years, as the government was determined to destroy
every trace of " superstitious popish books of
church service." Records extend over many years,
and show that the Queen's searchers sought out
with unswerving diligence, not only " books for use
in the papistical idolatry," but also " Latin books
of private superstition." A few examples culled
from many hundreds will be sufficient to prove
the zeal of the Queen's inquisitorial methods. In
1561, the parishes of the county of Norfolk[1] were
searched for " books of devotion and service forbidden by law," and the names of those who
possessed them were demanded for further dealings. In the same year the Protestant prelates
met at Lambeth, and made an order that " all old
service-books, grails, antiphonars, &c., be utterly
defaced and abolished."[2] This order was generally
enforced. In 1565, the parishes of Derbyshire,
Warwickshire, Staffordshire and Worcester were
searched to find " Mass books, portesses and all
other books of the Latin Service."[3] In 1569, the
private houses in the parishes of Norfolk and
Suffolk were searched for " old church service

[1] *Articles* (Brit. Mus.), 5155. aa. 8.
[2] *Corpus Christi MSS.* (Cambridge) cvi. 422.
[3] *State Papers Domestic*, xxxvi. 41.

books,"[1] and in the same year a similar search was carried out in all the parishes of Staffordshire and Worcestershire.[2] As late as 1571 many old service books survived, especially in the Northern parishes, and in that year a diligent enquiry was made for them in every parish north of Chester and Hull.[3] Even London and the neighbourhood of the government's central activity were not free from them. The city parishes were searched in 1572,[4] and this search was extended to the northern parishes in Kent in the same year.[5] In 1569, the churchwardens of the counties bordering on Wales were ordered to see that books of superstition were destroyed. These examples will be sufficient to illustrate the diligence of the government, but they suggest questions: Why was the search so necessary, and why was it extended over such a number of years? Other documents supply the answer.[6] Many of the books, and indeed other ornaments of the church, were hidden away in private houses, or in secret places[7] in the churches, as the people hoped " for the Mass and idolatrous service again." It is clear, however, that the old parish churches were practically gutted from end to end. Doors, lead on the roofs, and bells, were torn down and sold. The altars were removed. The roods, lofts and screens, were burned with the vestments and books. Pews and seats and carved

[1] *Second Ritual Report*, App. E., p. 404.
[2] *Lansdowne MSS.*, xi. f. 204.
[3] *Second Ritual Report*, App. E., p. 407.
[4] *Articles* (Brit. Mus.), 698. h. 20, 10).
[5] *Guest MSS.*, vii. f. 118.
[6] *E.g., State Papers Domestic*, lx. 71.
[7] *Ibid.*, xxxvi. 41.

woodwork went to make frames for beds, or
supports for bridges. The windows were broken
and often remained so. Images were destroyed
and their niches whitewashed over. We entered
at the beginning of this chapter the House of God,
magnificent as far as parochial ability could make
it. At this point we leave it desolate and outraged,
no longer a church fit for Catholic worship, but
a pathetic ruin. The four walls stood, and the
Reformers now began to furnish them for the new
religion.

The reign began with a religious compromise,
and for a time this fact influenced the furniture of
the parish churches. For some purpose or other
the Queen would have wished a dignified ceremonial, and the Royal Chapel at the beginning
of the reign was perhaps the only place in the kingdom where any attempt was made to carry out the
strict requirements of the law. As we have seen,
devastation more or less reigned supreme, and
finally the ornaments of the parish churches
reached the lowest level of decency. For a little
over a year the bishops made an effort to substitute
the use of a cope at the Communion Service
throughout their dioceses, instead of the old vestments. This effort proved a failure, and the cope,
if used at all, was confined to cathedral and colle-
giate churches whose history lies outside the scope
of this survey. The forces of Protestantism, as
represented by the returned exiles, were in the final
analysis too strong for anything like a conservative
policy. The Queen gradually receded from her
position as the Reformation movement made head-

way, and the reign was not many months old before we find the extreme ideals of the episcopate as a body coming so emphatically to the front that even the wearing of a surplice became a stumbling block to many as a relic of " papistry and ignorance." The dreary history is worn almost threadbare, but Elizabethan Puritanism seems at least to have been more logical in the end than the Established Church, within which it did much to make itself felt. There is one feature, however, of the question which has largely escaped notice. In no small degree the parochial clergy were their own guides, and there were at times divergences in the furniture of the parish churches as well as divergences of teaching, which bear no small resemblance to those in modern Anglicanism. Our study, then, must be modified by keeping these facts in mind : but it is possible, however, to present a view of the inside of an Elizabethan parish church which will be true to facts.

When the stone altars were removed—and their very foundations went with them[1]—it became necessary to furnish the churches with some suitable and congruous place to celebrate the Communion Service of the Book of Common Prayer. In the early months of the reign the altars were removed amid scenes of violence and irreverence, and it is clear that the Queen was moved[2] to approve of their destruction, although the strict letter of the law provided for their continuance. The Queen's conversion on this matter at once bore fruit, and

---

[1] Cf. *Second Ritual Report*, App. E., p. 411.
[2] Strype, *Annals*, I. i. 237.

an order[1] was issued in 1559 to the effect that the
altars should be taken down under the oversight
of the clergyman and churchwardens, in order to
avoid riotous behaviour, and that a decent Holy
Table should be set up in every church in the
place where the altar stood.   This Table was not
to be fixed to the floor, orders being given that it
should be moved about the chancel for the con-
venience of the clergyman and communicants
during the Communion Service.   Indeed it would
seem that the Table was often moved[2] outside the
chancel into the body of the church when there
were many communicants, and the Catholic
champions were not slow to notice this.[3]   " This
day your Communion Table is placed in the midst
of the choir, the next removed into the body of
the church."   Nor were their statements based on
mere hearsay.   A government survey[4] for the
diocese of London noted the same facts.   The
exact make-up of the Table is a matter of debate,
but the same survey noticed that " in some places
the Table is joined, in others it standeth upon
trestles."   The details were left to the decision
of the local churchwardens and clergymen.   No
lighted candles stood on it, as far as can be dis-
covered, during the celebration, when it was
covered with " a fair linen cloth " according to the
rubric in the Prayer Book.   Diligent efforts were
made to protect it from irreverence when it was
not in use, as it often stood covered with dust, or

[1] Gee and Hardy, p. 439.
[2] *Petyt MSS*. (Inner Temple) 538. 38. ff. 223 and 538.
47. f. 545.
[3] Dorman, *Proof of Certain Articles* (1564), p. 120
(Brit. Mus. 3932. f.).
[4] *Lansdowne MSS*., viii. f. 16.

became the receptacle for hats and cloaks. In
1561, a Royal Order[1] was issued that it should be
covered with " some covering of silk, buckram or
such like for the keeping clean of the fair linen
cloth, at the cost of the parish." This order was
treated with some contempt. The Government
survey already quoted, proves that " in some places
the Table hath a carpet, in other places it hath
not." This divergency applies to the year 1565;
but there is ample evidence to prove that the Holy
Table was little cared for during the reign. Thus,
for example, the churchwardens in all the parishes
north of Chester and Hull were ordered[2] as late
as 1571 to see that the Holy Table was decently
covered, and this order was extended to the Fen
parishes in the same year,[3] and repeated in 1574.[4]
On the other hand, local differences often erred
on the other side, and in not a few cases Catholic
ornaments for the Holy Table were retained. Some
of them, as in the parishes of Norfolk, were frequently " decked like an altar."[5] Of course
Tabernacles disappeared and the wall behind the
Table, where the principal image of the Church
had stood in Catholic days according to Canon Law
and diocesan instructions,[6] was ornamented with
" Tables of God's precepts,"[7] or " other godly
sentences of Scripture."[8] After what has been
said of vestments, crosses and altar vessels, little
remains to be noted about the new Holy Table.

[1] *Brit. Mus.* C. 25. g. 18.
[2] *Second Ritual Report*, App. E., p. 411.
[3] *Ibid.*, p. 406. [4] *Brit. Mus.* 5155. a. 20 (1).
[5] *Ibid.*, 5155. aa. 8.
[6] Lyndwood, *Provinciale* (1697), p. 253. *Pole MS. Register*, f. 34.
[7] See note 1.
[8] *State Papers Domestic*, xxxvi. 41. (1).

A surplice was a barely tolerated minimum of
decency, the crucifix disappeared, and communion
cups with covers took the place of the old chalices
and patens, with " two comely pots of pewter to
fetch wine, being no tavern pots."[1]   Censers and
Sanctus bells had no place in the new régime, and
the new Holy Table stood grim and unbeautiful
in strange contrast with the glorious altars of
Catholic England, and round it there sat not unfrequently the communicants on rude benches.[2]

The early zeal for reform had to a large extent
broken down any partition between the chancel and
the nave of the church. The Rood and its accom-
panying figures, which had been restored to a large
extent under Mary,[3] were at once destroyed as
" idols and false gods." Zeal, however, in this
connexion outran the intentions of the Government,
and in the vast majority of churches the chancel
screen disappeared to provide wood for the bonfires
of church furniture, and the rood-loft was also torn
down in the unrestrained desire to " get away with
popish gear." A survey of the churchwardens'
accounts goes to show that in a few cases where
the wood was not burned, it was sold and used for
bedposts, bridges, the new Holy Tables, or church
pews. The government, however, were not prepared to have the churches turned into one long
building as had been aimed at under Edward VI,

[1] *Brit. Mus.* 5155. a. 20 (1).
[2] See for example the Churchwardens' accounts for the
parish of Yatton, where "forms for Communion" were
purchased in 1559, and compare the Royal Survey of 1565
(*op. cit.*), where it was noted that some of the communicants sat.
[3] Wriothesley, *Chronicle*, ii. p. 131, and compare *British
Museum Injunctions*, 1026. e. 14 (2).

and they issued an injunction restraining the excess
of reforming enthusiasm. The lofts were " trans-
posed and so altered that the upper part of the
same, with the (loft), be quite taken down to the
upper parts of the vaults and the beam running in
length over the said vaults by putting some convenient crest upon the said beam towards the
church." The result aimed at was to produce
" a comely partition betwixt the chancel and the
church," and this could be obtained either by re-
modelling the old screen as suggested, or building
a new one " in joiner's work." Many of these
screens still remain, doubtless owing to the fact
that episcopal injunctions with regard to their pre-
servation were issued to the different parishes
during the entire reign. On the other hand these
orders must have been largely neglected, as the
proportion of pre-Reformation screens, or new
Elizabethan screens, is comparatively small.

Even the fonts did not escape the attention of
the Reformers. The clergymen who were infected
with extreme Puritanism seem to have considered
them as too " infested with papistry," and many
of them were destroyed or removed, even though
the doctrine of Baptism did not come prominently
into dispute under Elizabeth. The government
interfered to preserve them, as it had done in the
case of the chancel screens, but only a slight
success seems to have followed their efforts. Thus,
it is not uncommon to find that the clergy
introduced new ornaments into the church in the
form of basins, bowls, and dishes, and were with
difficulty compelled to use the fonts.[1]

[1] See for example, *British Museum Articles*, T. 1015 (1).

Little more needs to be said with regard to Elizabethan church furniture; but certain characteristic items remain to be noted. Side by side in the churches lay a copy of the English Bible, of the Prayer Book, of the *Paraphrases* of Erasmus, of the Royal Injunctions, and of various official directions and orders. To these were added from time to time some works of the Reformers, especially of Bishop Jewel, a metrical Psalter, The Books of Homilies and Canons, and a Table of Prohibited Degrees in Marriage. Parish Registers lay in the vestry. The pulpit stood in a prominent place. A new poor-box witnessed to the growing distress. A seat in the body of the church was frequently provided for the clergyman while saying the service. The windows were chiefly filled with plain glass. The walls were whitewashed and bricked up where images had stood. Ancestral tombs remained, but as often as not the effigies on them were hacked and broken. A bell called the people to prayer or warned them of the approaching death of some neighbour. Everything in the church from the chancel to the door spoke of reform and change. The interiors of the churches reflected the introduction of the new religion in every detail of furniture, and before the reign closed they were so completely transformed that only imagination could connect them with the beauty of Catholic worship and the traditions of Catholic piety.[1]

[1] As the evidence for the general furniture mentioned in this paragraph is drawn from the various documents which have been referred to already in this chapter, I have not thought it necessary to give references.

CHAPTER V.

THE PARISH SERVICES AND CEREMONIES.

IN order to understand the parochial services in Elizabeth's reign, and to form some idea of the ceremonial connected with them on the part of both clergy and laity, it will be necessary to obtain a cursory acquaintance with the Book of Common Prayer as issued in the first year of the reign under the Act of Uniformity. This Prayer Book was the standard of ritual and ceremonial, and any digression from it was punishable by law. In addition, it represents such a difference from pre-Reformation rites and ceremonies, that a short survey of it is essential before considering Elizabethan worship. Doubtless in many parishes old methods lingered and old ceremonies survived, and in many, Reformation extremes nullified the new regulations. To these we shall refer later. But the fact that there were differences in the carrying out of the parochial services need not prevent us from obtaining a sufficiently broad view, which will adequately represent the religious life of the nation in public worship. In England it is true that before the Reformation there were various " uses "; but it may be said that under Mary the use of Salisbury was practically universal throughout the kingdom. Even the differences between the various " uses " were never so pronounced as to lead anyone to think that he was assisting at anything except Catholic worship. The great outstanding features were the same, and Mass under the use of Hereford or Lincoln was, so far as the laity were concerned, practically identical with that under the use of Salisbury. It is well to bear this in mind, as it was not unfrequently asserted during the reign, that pre-Reformation differences justified contemporary deviations from the Prayer Book. We have heard something of this in modern times.

The Elizabethan Prayer Book provided for Morning and Evening Prayer in " a loud voice," consisting of a general confession of sin, canticles and psalms, lessons from the Old and New Testaments, and various collects. The Litany was ordered for Sundays, Wednesdays, and Fridays. The order for the administration of the Lord's Supper consisted of Prayers, the Ten Commandments, Collects for the Queen and the day, Epistle, Gospel and Creed, a sermon, Homily, or Exhortation, and a form of Consecration. There was no mention of the Saints or the Holy Dead. The people were ordered to give in their names beforehand when they desired to receive Communion, which they were expected to do three times a year. They were to receive kneeling and in their hands, and there was to be no celebration without communicants. No orders were given as to a daily or weekly carrying out of the rite. Baptism was to be administered on Sundays and Holydays. Godfathers and godmothers were retained. The child was to be dipped in the font, or, if too weak, to be sprinkled, and the sign of the cross made on its forehead by the clergyman. Children were to

be brought to the bishop for Confirmation as soon
as they could say the Lord's Prayer, Apostles'
Creed, the Ten Commandments and the Protestant
Catechism in English. Banns of Marriage were
to be published on three consecutive Sundays or
Holydays, and provision was made for Holy Communion at the Marriage ceremony. The Burial
Service consisted of sentences of Scripture, Psalms,
and a chapter from St. Paul's Epistle to the
Corinthians; prayers were not offered for the repose
of the soul of the departed, and no celebration
of the Holy Communion for the dead took place.
A thanksgiving service for women after childbirth
was to be said by the clergyman, and they were
to receive Communion if convenient. Finally, a
" commination against sinners " was to be read
at different times during the year. The vestments
as ordered in the first year of Edward VI were
retained. This outline covers the scope of the
Book, so far as public services were concerned.
Certain features at once strike us. Firstly, the
Holy Communion was no longer a service of
obligation on Sundays or various Saints' days.
Secondly, there were few directions to guide clergy
and people in ceremonial, in spite of the fact that
the Statute Law implied that the book was a complete guide in this respect. Thirdly, Morning and
Evening Prayer were held up as the norm of
Sunday worship, and fourthly, the whole book represented a violent breaking away from Catholic
rites and ceremonies. Only by an extreme stretch
of the imagination could it be connected in any
way with the worship which had gone on in

England for centuries before the Reformation. It was destined to be, with few changes in later centuries, a new and permanent contribution to Reformation service-books. From these features certain results might follow. The idea of sacrificial worship might disappear, and those who clung to the old Faith might not easily be won to subjective worship. There might be a disposition to follow private opinion in ceremonial. In the retention of the old vestments, and in forms of prayers, the wholesale reformers might find points of stumbling, while the conservative people in the parishes might find the book a " hugger mugger " or " mingle mangle," and treat it as such. As the history develops we shall see how every one of these results took place. As religious matters stood in England during the reign, the Book contained germs of discord, and only the application of the severest orders, and the most diligent diocesan injunctions, could win for it parochial acceptance. In the first half of the reign we find numerous documents enforcing it on Catholic and Protestant alike: before the reign was over the best and most religious Protestants refused it, and the reign closed in a wounded cry of offended Puritanism.

It will facilitate our survey if we divide the Prayer Book services into two groups. Firstly, the less frequent: Baptism, Matrimony, Confirmation, Burial of the Dead, Churching of Women, and the Commination. Secondly, the more common: Morning and Evening Prayer, and the Holy Communion. The latter service indeed became uncommon enough as the reign progressed, but there were efforts made to bring about frequent celebrations, and our review will be easier if we follow the division outlined, and accept the spirit of diocesan rule. Before reviewing each service it must be understood that the study is based on documents covering the widest areas, and reflecting life in the greatest number of parishes. Doubtless, minute research among the documents of different archdeaconries would reveal details which might modify the picture; and, doubtless, the history of special parishes would provide illustrations of local customs and local peculiarities. It has been thought best, however, to eliminate any account of parochial worship and ceremonial belonging to one or two parishes. However interesting such accounts may be in themselves, they would only serve, if worked up into a general picture, to obscure history, and to render still more difficult a subject sufficiently complicated in its general breadth. Thus, then, as we consider each Prayer Book Service in detail, the review will be based on evidence which belongs to a sufficient number of dioceses to make it possible to say that the history of each service is drawn from the general records of Elizabethan parish life.

Baptism was to be administered at the font by the parish clergyman. Godfathers and godmothers must stand for the child, and declare their belief on behalf of the child in the Apostles' Creed. The sign of the cross was the only ceremony. There was no anointing. These were the provisions. Very early in the reign it became

clear that there would be trouble. When Parker[1]
was making preparations in 1563 for the first
Convocation of the new régime, he requested his
brethren to furnish him with lists of reforms which
they considered necessary. Three of these papers
survive, and to them may be added some petitions
of the Lower House. In these documents requests
were made that the " sign of the cross " be done
away with in Baptism as it was " very superstitious," and that the answering of sponsors should
be discontinued. Incidentally, they disclose an
abuse which had grown up. A demand was made
that baptism by women should be forbidden—this
does not refer to baptism in case of emergency,
but to common custom. Further light is thrown
on the question by the fact that a report was made
to Parker in 1564, that some of the parochial clergy
wished the father to christen his own child, or that
he should be admitted to be chief godfather, while
on the other hand many desired that there should
be seven godfathers. Actual " reform " had
already advanced, and in several parishes the font
was removed, and a great bowl provided with
" Baptisme " painted on the outside.[2] These and
additional changes were notified in the following
year to the Government: " Some baptize in a font,
others in a basin; some sign with the cross, others
sign not."[3] A closer study of parochial documents provides further illustrations of departure
from the orders contained in the Prayer Book. In

[1] W. P. M. Kennedy, *Parker*, 174.
[2] Strype, *Parker*, i. 30.
[3] *Lansdowne MSS.*, viii. f. 16.

spite of an injunction from the Government[1] forbidding the removal of the font, the use of basins,
and any alteration of the legal arrangement
about godfathers and godmothers, there is evidence
that in many parishes the law was a dead letter.
For example, the general use of English was not
adhered to in the service; vessels of varied kinds
and often those employed in household and
domestic duties took the place of the font;[2] oil
and chrism were continued;[3] many refused to
allow their children to be baptized in their own
parish churches or according to the Prayer Book
rite.[4] In places, some one not in Holy Orders
baptized publicly in the parish church.[5] Frequently the godparents were closely examined on
their adherence to Reformation doctrine,[6] but this
custom was not universal. Ceaseless efforts were
made to bring about conformity, but the evidence
goes to prove that the many variations noted continued throughout the entire reign. The position
may be summed up somewhat as follows: in
some churches, the Baptismal rite and ceremonies
provided in the New Service Book were followed;
in some, this rite was mixed up with Catholic
practices; in some, the clergyman followed his own
private ideas, or those of the parents; and in not

---

[1] *Royal Order* (Brit. Mus.), C. 25. g. 18.

[2] See for example, *Brit. Mus.* 5155. de 24.   A sketch
of such a " bowl " or " dish " is in James Parker, *The
Ornaments of the Rubric*, p. 54 (1899).

[3] *Second Ritual Report*, App. E., pp. 407, 411.

[4] *Brit. Mus.* 5155. a. 20 (1), *Lansdowne MSS.*, xi.
f. 204.

[5] *Ritual Report, op. cit.*

[6] *Horne MS. Register*, f. 67.

F

a few cases, where sacramental teaching had gradually degenerated, Baptism was not administered at all.   Minor details need not delay us. It is sufficiently clear that uniformity did not exist.

With regard to four of the first group of Prayer Book services under consideration—Confirmation, Matrimony, Churching of Women, and the Commination—there is no large number of documents extant to guide us.   Certain features, however, emerge which are worthy of record.   Thus, while the Prayer Book specified no age, orders were issued in 1565 to the parish clergy of Derbyshire and Staffordshire to present for Confirmation all children over seven years.[1]   On the other hand this age is the youngest recorded.   In 1561 the Bishops agreed[2] that no one should be confirmed before the age of twelve or thirteen and this episcopal decision seems to have been widely enforced.[3] In connexion with the preparation for Confirmation, certain instructions took place in the churches which may be considered at this point.   On Sundays and Holydays the Catechism was taught for half an hour before Evening Prayer.[4]   In places the time was changed and lengthened,[5] and children over six years of age were compelled to attend.[6]   In cases where the children could not come in before Evensong, two children were

---

[1] *State Papers Domestic*, xxxvi. 41 (3).
[2] W. P. M. Kennedy, *The Interpretations of the Bishops*, pp. 32, 41.
[3] *E.g.*, *Rochester MSS.*, vii. f. 98v (13).
[4] For example, see *Lansdowne MSS.*, xi. f. 204, *Second Ritual Report*, App. E., 406.
[5] For example, see *Brit. Mus.* 698. h. 20 (1).
[6] *Horne MS. Register, op. cit.*

examined after the first reading of Scripture for
the edification of their fellows and grown-up
neighbours.[1]   The duty of finding out those in
the parishes who did not know the Catechism de-
volved upon the churchwardens, and lists of the
ignorant were furnished by them to the parish
clergyman[2] — parents and guardians who refused
to help in this respect were reported to the authorities for correction.[3]   General neglect of catechizing
and confirmation, however, seems to have characterized the closing years of the reign, and Archbishop Whitgift complained in 1591 that his
brethren the Bishops " did generally begin to
neglect to confirm children."[4]   With regard to
Matrimony, consistent attempts were made to enforce the legal requirements, but certain orders not
contained in the Prayer Book were enforced.   For
example, no marriage was solemnized before six
o'clock in the morning in the summer, and seven
in the winter, " at what time the broad daylight
doth appear."[5]   None could be married outside
their own parish churches except by special permission, and until they passed a thorough examination on The Lord's Prayer, Creed, and Ten
Commandments, the Catechism being added in
certain parishes.[6]   The Churching of Women was
sometimes entrusted to lay readers,[7] although the
Prayer Book ordered that the parish minister

1 *State Papers, op. cit.* (6).
2 *E.g.,* Grindal, *Remains,* p. 123.
3 *Second Ritual Report,* App. E., p. 407.
4 *Whitgift MS. Register,* i. f. 181.
5 *Brit. Mus.* 5155. a. 8 (1).
6 See Grindal and *Brit. Mus., op. cit.*
7 *Petyt MSS.,* 538. 38. f. 223.

should perform the rite; nor were women
" churched " after giving birth to illegitimate
children, unless they " had done some penance for
their fault to the satisfaction of the congregation,
or at their coming to give thanks do openly
acknowledge their fault before the congregation
at the appointment of the minister by the Ordinary
or his deputy."[1] No provision was made in the
Prayer Book for such cases. The Commination or
Warning to Sinners was read at different times and
on different occasions in the parishes; but attempts
were made to regulate this reading. Thus, for
example, in all the parishes of Northern England
it was read between the Litany and Holy Communion on one of the Sundays before Easter, one
before Pentecost, and one before Christmas, in
addition to Ash Wednesday.

In considering the last service in the first division—the Burial of the Dead—we are confronted
with such a mass of varieties that it will only be
possible to select the most outstanding. It is
worthy of note that in this connexion a similar
wide departure from Protestant standards took
place under Edward VI, and it would seem that
the people clung closer to the old customs connected with burial than to anything else of Catholic
practice and tradition. Thus, for example, the
Prayer Book orders were disregarded by singing
psalms dirge-like,[2] by setting up lights round the
bier,[3] by setting down the body at wayside
crosses, or where they had stood, to say *De*

[1] *Second Ritual Report, op. cit.*
[2] *Brit. Mus.* 5155. aa. 8.
[3] *State Papers Domestic,* xxxvi. 41 (5).

Profundis,[1] and by ringing forth-fares. In places too, prayers for the dead with obits and dirges lingered,[2] and the Communion Service was turned into a Mass of Requiem.[3] The departures from the grim rite and ceremony provided in the Prayer Book continued for many years, and the strictest diocesan administration did not succeed in completely eradicating them. In spite of all episcopal efforts, the burial customs of Catholic times lingered after Elizabeth's death in the remote parishes of the North and West. In connexion with no service in this division were larger difficulties experienced in producing conformity. The human heart seemed to revolt against Protestant teaching in this respect, and the Government found it difficult to dragoon natural instincts.

We need not survey the customs connected with Morning and Evening Prayer, as these services did not admit of much variety. The minister wearing a " decent surplice with large sleeves " read the service in the chancel, or at a large desk or stool outside the chancel gates[4]—the latter being an episcopal arrangement agreeable to the Prayer Book rubrics. In connexion with these services, however, the sermon held a prominent place, although the Prayer Book only provided for it after the Creed in the Holy Communion. Perhaps this inclusion of the sermon, and a somewhat wide refusal to wear the surplice, were the only points in which Morning and Evening Prayer departed

[1] *Ibid.* (17); *Second Ritual Report*, App. E., p. 412.
[2] *Parker MS. Register*, i. f. 302.
[3] *State Papers, op. cit.*
[4] *Second Ritual Report*, App. E., p. 404.

from the letter of the law. The sermons were not as a rule edifying. When the Government, by means of an elaborate system of fining and spying, had filled the churches, care was taken to see that every parish pulpit was carefully tuned to the new system, and that the Pope was diligently denounced by licensed preachers, who were men carefully tried by the Government officials. It is a mistake to think that all the parish clergy were licensed or permitted to preach. Licenses were confined to those whose Protestantism had undergone official sanction, especially with regard to the " Bishop of Rome and all his superstitious usurpations." For the rest, they confined themselves to reading printed Homilies on the dullest points of contemporary controversy. This denunciation of the Pope became part and parcel of the parochial system, evidently on the principle that some part at least of regular denunciation would find its way to the hearts of the people, bereft of priests and Catholic literature. Thus, for example, in 1565,[1] the parishes of Kent were provided with special preachers " to speak against the supremacy of the Pope and to maintain the Queen's Majesty to be Supreme Governor of this Church." Throughout the parishes of Norfolk "the just taking away of the Pope's usurped power " was prescribed in 1561 as the sole subject for a quarterly discourse.[2] In 1569, many of the parishes in Winchester diocese[3] were brought into line when six annual sermons

[1] *Rochester MSS.*, vii. f. 98v.
[2] *Brit. Mus.* 5155. aa. 8.
[3] *Winchester MSS.*, f. 67 (1569).

were ordered, " to confirm the Queen's Majesty's royal authority in all causes ecclesiastical against the late usurped power of the Bishop of Rome." It was little to be wondered at that the solid body of Puritans called out for reformation of morals and less controversy. Elizabethan sermons were not meant to edify. The pulpit became the parochial centre for official comments on the Act of Supremacy. Church and State were never more happily wedded.

In conclusion, there remains the service of "The Lord's Supper or Holy Communion." We have already noticed in broad outline the Elizabethan dealings with vestments, altar-vessels, candlesticks, bells, and all the other necessaries for the Mass. The subject has produced a literature of its own, to which wisdom would not wish to add. Varieties in administration were almost infinite, and the Government survey so frequently quoted gives some idea of them. " The Table standeth in the body of the church in some places, in others it standeth in the chancel. In some places the Table standeth altar-like distant from the wall a yard, some others in the midst of the chancel north and south. In some places the Table is joined, in others it standeth upon trestles. In some the Table hath a carpet, in others it hath none. Some (administer) with surplice and cope,[1] some with surplice alone, others with none, some with chalice, some with communion cup, others without a com-

[1] I adhere to the reading " cope " in spite of criticism. I have no reason to recall what I have written elsewhere (*Interpretations of the Bishops*, p. 19, note). The document is in *Lansdowne MSS.*, viii. f. 16.

munion cup, some with unleavened bread, some
with leavened. Some receive kneeling, some
standing, others sitting." It can hardly be believed
that variety could go beyond this summary, but that
it did so is abundantly evident. The *minutiae* of
differences would fill a large volume. Sometimes
there were communicants, sometimes none.[1] Sometimes there was a celebration once a month, sometimes every Sunday.[2] Sometimes the minister
" counterfeited the Popish Mass," or " crossed and
breathed over the sacramental bread and wine,
showing the same to the people to be worshipped
and adored," and " decked the Lord's Table like
an altar."[3]   It is unnecessary to broaden the
picture. Infinite variety was the rule, and private
opinion the only authority.

The stereotyped round of parochial services—
dull in spite of variety—did not long escape a
significant change. In the earlier years of the
reign, parochial meetings were held for mutual
conference over Scripture. These were connived at
by the Government and encouraged by some of the
bishops. After the Puritan crisis of 1566, these
meetings became the object of suspicion, and this
was further emphasized by the position taken up
by Cartwright and other extremists, who described
the Prayer Book as " culled and picked out of that
popish dungheap, the Mass Book, full of all
abominations." The Queen finally lost patience,
and ordered Parker, almost at the close of his work,

[1] Cf. *Guest MSS.*, vii. f. 98 (6).
[2] *Ibid.* (1). (2).
[3] *Second Ritual Report*, App. E., p. 407, and cf. *Brit.
Mus.*, 5155. aa. 8 (1).

to suppress the " vain exercises of prophesyings,"
as these unconventional parochial meetings were
called. The matter became complicated when the
Bishop of London and several of the Council
advised disregard of the royal order. The Queen,
however, seems to have attacked only the parishes
in Norfolk, as the prophesyings continued till
Parker's death in the northern parishes of Kent
" greatly to the comfort of God's church." [1] In
later years wider efforts were made at suppression,
especially in Worcestershire,[2] and the Queen commanded them to be discontinued throughout
England.[3] She noted the parochial divisions which
they produced, and the ideals of Tudor statecraft
did not include religious toleration.

Parochial life, then, so far as public worship was
concerned, may be summed up as disintegrated and
drastic. It afforded a pathetic contrast to the high-
sounding conceptions of Reform which had
heralded the new era. The Reformation was
ushered in amid glowing guarantees of a higher
life and a sincerer approach to God. But of these
no sign had appeared. The parish services called
the people to no Christian effort. They provided
examples for a contempt of authority, for a policy
of *laissez faire*, and they encouraged religious
bitterness and controversy. It was little wonder
that parochial life degenerated in one aspect into
religious warfare. There was scarcely a parish
in England which did not reflect in its every-day
life something of the variety which went on within

[1] See W. P. M. Kennedy, *Parker*, pp. 278 ff.
[2] Strype, *Whitgift*, i. 163.
[3] *Cotton MSS.*, Cleop. F. 2. f. 2877.

the parish churches. On all sides parties were formed on lines of religious differences. Not merely did theology provide a line of demarcation, but such petty details as a " square cap," or a " surplice," were sufficient to produce serious parochial friction. It is an unedifying picture, from which the best men of the age turned in pathetic disgust. We must, however, consider the history of these opposing forces in parochial life.

CHAPTER VI.

PAROCHIAL PURITANISM.

FROM what we have already seen of parish life under Elizabeth, it will be no surprise to find that it was not one of happiness and content. The Tudor theory of religion had let loose forces which were by no means easily controlled, and every-day existence in a parish reflected the evil influences of these forces in unedifying disputes, family feuds and, at times, unseemly disturbances. It is almost true to say that each parish was divided into three religious camps—Extreme Reformers, Reformers, and Catholics—and that the last were further divided into three groups, into which they were admirably classed by a contemporary preacher:[1] "Of Papists there are three kinds. The ' open Papist ' which dwelleth among us and for-saketh our communion . . . . protesting that we

[1] *Lansdowne MSS.*, 945. f. 172.

are departed from the Catholic Church and therefore that they may not in conscience join with us. The second sort are ' fleeing Papists ' which fleeing over the seas . . . . or return to steal away the hearts of subjects from the Prince . . . The third the ' cunning Papist ' which can hide himself under the colour of loyalty and obedience to the laws, and will needs be accounted a faithful, true and good subject, and yet carrieth in his bosom the same persuasion that the other do, and for fear of danger or discredit, they are contented to obey the law."

We need not delay our study by considering the average Reformer. He was sufficiently contented to accept the changes, and to observe the Common Prayer Book. During the reign there is little evidence of his disturbing influence in parochial life. He sought peace and quietness, and as a rule he wisely attended his parish church and kept himself apart from the extremes, as he considered them, of Catholicism and Puritanism. He was the product of Elizabethan statecraft, which aimed to build up a national religion on the principles of a *via media*. Infinite care was exerted by the Government to protect the growth of his opinions, and to increase his influence. He became, by minute supervision and an anxious oversight, the typical Established Churchman, content to take his religion from the Crown and Parliament, to shun anything like extremes, and to value Parker's " decent moderation." Such ideals, making no severe demands, and witnessing not only to loyalty to God but to the Government, were typically

Tudor; the Government, however, taking first place.
To build up loyalty to the Throne, and, incidentally,
to connect it with religion was the palpable aim,
and as the reign advanced most Englishmen were
content to accept the ideal, at least outwardly. But
this position was not arrived at without strife and
controversy. It is obvious after our consideration
of the clergy, that there could not be immediate
consolidation among a people whose religious
leaders were perverts, foreign extremists and
Scotch exiles. Any success which the ideal attained
was reached when another generation of clergymen
grew up, and even this success was never destined
to be permanent or influential. The reasons for
such success as was gained hardly come within the
scope of our work. However, it may reasonably
be said that if there were no conviction expressed
in public actions there would be compulsion, and
if there were no compulsion necessary, the Government concluded there was conviction. Elizabeth
and her councillors were determined to build up
an England at unity with itself—one in politics
and in at least external religion. The materials
were Puritans, moderate Protestants, and Catholics.
The middle course of moderate Protestantism was
aimed at as the ideal of " Tudor Catholicism," and
the extremes of " Precisians " and " Recusants "
felt the firm hand of the Government as their position came into prominence.

The Puritan may well be considered first, as he
was the first with whom the Government dealt.
From the very beginning, extreme Reformers were
full of hopes, and as the reign advanced they

carried on such an active propaganda that their adherents increased throughout the country. Behind them lay the enthusiasm and zeal of their friends abroad, and a ceaseless correspondence went on between them, which helped to fan the flame of nonconformity among the people. Books were imported, in which the system of religion erected at Geneva [1] was unreservedly praised as one " through which godliness was wonderfully advanced and error mightly beaten down." In Geneva, " heresy and strange pestiferous doctrine were narrowly seen into," and the ecclesiastical policy " taken out of the Gospel of Jesus Christ was ordained and established, with the sound of the trumpet and great bell." The fair picture of Continental reform was set forth in enticing detail and influenced in no small degree parochial opinion. Before very long it was clear that there was growing up in the country a strong body which was determined to drive reform to an excess beyond the Government's ideal. This body had merely accepted the Elizabethan Settlement, strong in the hope that it would soon receive the full impress of Protestant opinion. They determined to reform the Reformation in the Established Church, and to educate the people to such a degree in Continental Protestantism that every trace of " papistical idolatry " would be banished from the fair heritage of the Established Church where providentially " harbour was now granted to the afflicted members of Christ's Body."[2] It would be

[1] See for example, *The Laws and Statutes of Geneva* (Brit. Mus. 1127. b. 22).

[2] Sternfield and Hopkins, *Psalter*, p. 401 (1562), *Ibid.*, C. 25. g. 3.

foolhardy to dispute the sincerity of the Puritans
—they firmly believed in their vocation and they
were prepared to suffer for it. Strength came with
active work in various districts, and when the storm
of Government disapproval broke over the party
in 1566, it included in its ranks adherents drawn
from many parishes. Some idea of its position
may be gained from the fact that a motion
for further extreme reform failed to pass in the
Convocation of 1563 by only one vote, and that a
proxy one. Thus the clergy of England south of
Hull and Chester were evenly divided, and we may
conclude that each division of them represented a
considerable body of the laity. The history of the
rise of Elizabethan Puritanism is so voluminous
that it is almost impossible to touch the subject
without doing injustice to it. Broadly speaking,
the Puritans appealed to Scripture, not merely on
theological questions, but for directions in the
minutest details of ceremonial. Round such a
position the official battle opened in the spring of
1566, with the result that many of the clergy were
deprived, being " killed in their souls for this pollu-
tion " of Prayer Book decency—a day when " the
gracious knot of Christian charity was broken."[1]
Tumults at once broke out, and Holy Week was
disfigured by disgraceful scenes. Extremists
closed the church doors against conforming congregations, and loudly boasted that they would not
wear the surplices or " porters' coats " as they

---

[1] For this opening scene see *Earl MSS.* (*University
Library, Cambridge MSS.* Mm. i. 29.), and *Parker Correspondence,* Nos. ccv.-vii.-ix.-x.

called them.[1] Immediately literary warfare began, and the parochial life was further disturbed by an inflow of controversial literature. At first no new position was maintained, but as the literary conflict advanced it became clearer that the principles of Puritanism lay deeper than " the surplice, that hypocritical opinion of holiness." [2] Out of the painful monotony of old arguments emerged the clearcut and far-reaching statement " that neither prince nor prelate may by the word of God make ecclesiastical laws to bind men's consciences under the pain of deadly sin to keep them." [3] Such a claim could only be received as a warning that the point of attack would soon cease to be " surplices " or " popish relics," and would become a wholesale onslaught on the established ministry and the rites and ceremonies of the Prayer Book. In addition, this Puritan conception of " prince and prelate " was in complete disagreement with the Tudor ideal, and if persisted in must of necessity make for actual disintegration in the State religion. From the crisis of 1566 may be traced a clear dividing line. Parish life, so far as the Protestant elements were concerned, broke from that date into two distinct parties. Puritanism slowly but surely found that, being unable to reform the Establishment, it must seek to realize its conscientious convictions outside the Elizabethan Church. Almost immediately many of the London clergy determined to

---

[1] *Ibid.*, ccxi.-xiii.-xv.

[2] *To my Loving Brethren that are troubled about the Popish Apparel* (Brit. Mus. C. 37. d. 46 (5) (6)).

[3] *The Fortress of the Fathers* (Brit. Mus. C. 37. d. 46. (3)).

provide their people with separate congregations,[1] and meetings for Puritan worship spread from the city to the woods and lanes of different country parishes. When Parliament met in 1571, Puritanism had grown strong enough to demand, through Puritan members, far-reaching reform. Though the attempt was abortive, it illustrates the advance of Puritan opinions among the people. The literature of the following year provides further evidence, and also discloses the real tenets of the party: There was " no warrant in Scripture for the three orders of the ministry as used in the Established Church "; ministers should be chosen by the people; Articles, Homilies, Injunctions, and the Service Book were contrary to the good order of the Reformation as accepted in Scotland. This *Admonition to Parliament* was bought up with eagerness, the first edition being sold out almost immediately, and in three months three further editions were exhausted.[2] Reply and counter-reply followed, and before the close of 1575, parochial Puritanism outside the Established Church was an accomplished fact. Voluntary associations arose here and there, where the scattered forces of parochial " Precisians " were strengthened by vigorous exhortation in the party's principles, and

[1] Strype, *Parker*, i. 480.

[2] Consult Brook, *Lives of the Puritans*. Neal's *History of the Puritans* is unhistorical and biassed. Dr. Brown's *English Puritans* gives a good outline of the Puritan position, but is disfigured by errors of fact, and is not based on any wide research. The Puritan tracts are admirably edited in Frere and Douglas, *Puritan Manifestoes*. See my *Parker*, chapters xiii., xiv., xvi., xviii., where the authorities are given in detail.

a " new model " was drawn up, Calvinistic in teaching, and comprehensively Continental in ritual and ceremonial.[1] The members of these associations, however, would not at this period have considered themselves outside the Established Church. They still hoped to erect Presbyterianism, or even Congregationalism, within that institution. The germ developed—the nonconformist within became the separatist without. The " Battle of the Books " grew fierce, not merely in London, but all over the country. At times it was soldierly warfare, at times cowardly sniping,[2] and in both respects it reflected two types of parochial protagonists—the deeply-in-earnest Puritan, and his sleek, underhand brother. The struggle rose and fell, as each paper campaign brought into the open more champions of the State Church and more zealots for the " godly discipline." The early months of 1589 marked the clearest issue between the opposing force. Bancroft, afterwards Archbishop of Canterbury, preached a sermon[3] on February 9th, the first Sunday after the adjournment of Parliament, in which he asserted that " the superiority of bishops over other clergy was *jure divino*." It was no longer a dispute between Presbyterianism

[1] See *State Papers Domestic*, lxxiii. 38.

[2] Compare *A brief and plain Declaration . . . for the Discipline and Reformation of the Church*, with the *Marprelate Tracts*. The former (in Brit. Mus.) is the most restrained statement of Puritanism during the reign. There is much of interest to be found in Pierce, *An Historical Introduction to the Marprelate Tracts* (1908), but this book ought not to be read without reading Dr. Frere's able criticism of it in the *English Historical Review* (vol. xxv. p. 338).

[3] In Hicks, *Tracts*.

G

and a form of ministry merely erected by the State: it became a vital theological question between a ministry derived from laymen, and a ministry at least claiming to be derived from the Apostles. Bancroft's sermon cleared the air, but it strengthened the Puritan warriors. From many a parish new auxiliary forces were drawn which had been content to accept the Episcopacy so long as it was a mere affair of civil government. Men now came out into the open who, while Puritans at heart, had tolerated the Established Church so long as the issue was not clearly defined as in Bancroft's discourse. Revelations were in store. Many parishes under Puritan clergy were managed on the lines of the Continental model as embodied in *The Book of Discipline*, to which the clergy had secretly subscribed. They educated their parishioners in their own religious tenets, and accepted their discipline from meetings of clergy —*classes* or synods—while adhering to the rule of the bishops as a matter of legal form. Prayer Book rites and ceremonies were swept away, and in not a few places the parishioners attended a Presbyterian form of worship in their own parish churches. Here and there distinct and separate congregations grew up, and Puritanism, whether within or without the Established Church, had become a distinct and recognized force in parish life before the close of the reign.

Before proceeding to discuss Catholicism in this connexion, it may be well to consider Elizabethan Puritanism from the point of view of some of its ideals. It is true that in many instances this new

national movement fell into the hands of leaders
who were illogical and incapable of weighing the
relative relationship of theology and the details
of worship, but there were many reasons why
Puritanism, even apart from its public leaders,
should gain ground. It appealed to the individualism of an age which was gradually losing patience
with any form of corporate religious life. The
bishops and clergy who maintained the Elizabethan
settlement did not as a rule carry with them the
love and esteem of their people. Grave scandals
in diocesan administration permeated through the
chicanery of new courts and officials to parochial
life. Simony, bribery and general corruption in
the government of the Church discounted the high-
sounding professions of both clergyman and
bishop. There was a widespread decay in honesty
and fair dealing: creed and character were
divorced as perhaps never before in the history
of England, and in the issue the Puritans took up
a reasonable position when they claimed that a
system which lent itself to widespread evils and
frequently connived at serious moral remissness,
had little claim to be called divine as had been
done by Bancroft. If the Elizabethan Puritan
could not understand, on account of his very religious constitution, the other opposing force in
parish life—Catholicism—he soon understood the
middle term—Moderate Reform—and he found it
as hateful as anything savouring of Rome, and this
because he understood it. He hated Catholicism
from the prejudices of his upbringing—he loathed
and despised Moderate Reform because he had

lived with it in friendship, and found it to be state-craft with a thin veneer of religion. The Puritans deserve the pity of history. They were the most conscientious Reformers of their day. They sought to serve God, and it was the irony of their position to seek such service in an age when the national religion, which claimed to control them, gave the lie to its professions. Judged from Tudor ideals, the Puritan—like his fellow in suffering, the Catholic—was a naughty fellow, a disturber of parochial love and national unity. Judged in the clearer atmosphere of religious conviction, he is not unworthy of the highest praise. It was his material misfortune to have had convictions in an age of opinions; it is his lasting fortune to have held his ground looking to an eternity of truth. He believed he possessed the truth, and as a consequence he was intolerant. Perhaps the Moderate Reformer might claim the same position; but the moral character of Elizabethan Puritanism and of Elizabethan Moderate Reform lie far apart. " Nothing surely can have contributed so much to the opportunities, the power, the zeal, the hopes of the Puritans, as did the neglect of duty in the Church. At such a time ignorance and inability among the clergy were serious enough, but avarice and plain indifference to the meaning of a spiritual change were far worse. . . . . In many a parish the minister could only struggle through the service, never preached, but read, perhaps four purchased sermons in the course of a year, or, it may be, had never resided in the place at all, and had he done so, might only have made matters

worse by the example of his vicious life."[1]
Puritanism was the outcome of the failure of the
State Church to make decent Christians.

The rise of Puritanism introduced another
element into parish life. Representing as it did a
disintegrating principle, the Government determined that it should be severely dealt with. From
the year 1566 to the close of the reign, there was
repression and persecution, varying in degree, but
consistent in purpose. On June 19th, 1567, the
sheriffs of London broke up a Puritan meeting and
took many prisoners. The serious state of affairs
throughout the country was not lost on Parliament.
In 1571, a bill was passed " for ministers to be of
sound religion,"[2] which enforced subscription to
the State Religion as embodied in the Thirty-nine
Articles of 1563. This Act was immediately put
into execution in the parishes of Northern Kent,[3]
and throughout England during the reign. Thus,
for example, enquiry was made in all the parishes
of Surrey and Hants in 1575 as to whether the
clergy[4] had carried out the statute. A similar
enquiry was held in the southern parts of Surrey
and Kent in 1585.[5] The documents quoted in this
connexion also dealt with the laity, forbidding
them to take part in any worship such as " conventicles," " expoundings " or " lectures " in
private houses conducted by " lay persons not
ordered according to the laws of this realm." Not

[1] Bishop Paget, *Introduction to Hooker's Ecclesiastical
Polity*, v. (1899).
[2] 13 Eliz. cap. xii.   [3] *Guest MSS.*, vii. f. 118.
[4] *Brit. Mus.* 5155. de 24 (1).
[5] *Whitgift MS. Register*, f. 116 v.

content with urging the bishops to repress Puritanism, the Ecclesiastical Commissioners issued orders
to the churchwardens of all parishes commanding
them to see that their clergy had fulfilled the new
obligations. When Whitgift became Primate the
severity of persecution against the Puritans was
increased. He immediately issued to his brethren
a series of orders aimed at the " Precisians," and
these were carried into every parish south of Hull
and Chester.[1] Tests were imposed on the parochial
clergy. They were forbidden to preach, read or
catechize in their churches, unless they celebrated
Holy Communion four times a year at least according to the strict letter of the Prayer Book, and
wearing a surplice. A new declaration for subscription was also sent round requiring every parish
minister solemnly to declare that he accepted the
sovereignty and rule of her Majesty in all ecclesiastical affairs; that there was nothing in the Prayer
Book and Ordering of Clergy contrary to the Word
of God; that he would faithfully adhere to the
established rites and ceremonies; that he believed
that the Thirty-nine Articles were agreeable to
Scripture, and that he would only use the official
translation of the Bible authorized by the episcopate. The result was ominous. Over two hundred
clergy failed to satisfy the requirements in six
counties alone—Kent, Sussex, Lincoln, Norfolk,
Suffolk and Essex. Even Cecil was moved to
protest, comparing Whitgift's action " to the in-
quisitors of Spain," and saying that the articles
for subscription " savoured of the Romish In-

[1] *Ibid.*, f. 97.

quisition." [1] But Whitgift defended his action as one necessary to national unity. Nor did repression stop here. Every printing-press in England outside London was closed except those connected with Oxford and Cambridge, and no book could be printed unless approved by the Archbishop or his deputies.[2] Active persecution continued everywhere, and Whitgift was strengthened by an Act of Parliament in 1593.[3] Everyone above the age of sixteen who refused to attend the State Church in his parish for one month, who seduced others or attended " Conventicles " or meetings under pretence of any " exercise of religion," should on conviction be imprisoned without fail until he conformed. If he persisted in his Puritan opinions, he must go into banishment. Thus the Puritan was placed in the awkward position of either accepting the national worship, or being banished from his home. There were many exiles for their convictions, and this Act laid in the issue the foundations of New England. The Government entirely failed to control the movement, as the succeeding reign proved. What concerns us, however, is that the opposing force of Puritanism was one of the chief characteristics of parochial religion during the reign, and that stern parochial repression dogged it at stated periods. This aspect of Elizabethan life has too often been obscured, and Protestantism presented as a united force against broken, disorganized Catholicism, to the consideration of which we now turn.

[1] Prothero, *Documents*, p. 213.
[2] *S. P. Domestic*, clxxxi. 48.
[3] 35 Eliz., cap. i.

CHAPTER VII.

PAROCHIAL CATHOLICISM.

WHEN the Elizabethan Settlement was arrived at, it presented at once a challenge to Catholicism. The first Parliament of the reign could not know that the Protestant party would split in the near future into two camps. The religion of England had been Catholic, and Catholicism was the earliest object of attack. It was a present evil, Puritanism a future possibility. If the germs of Puritanism were in the religious air, the Government hoped that they would be killed in an anti-Catholic campaign, and that a national ideal of religious unity would keep the atmosphere healthy. Puritanism, however, as we have seen, refused to die. It had reason to hope that the law only prescribed a minimum of reform, and that it did not exclude a better reform. The new bishops were not averse to further changes. Some of the most influential men about the Court were known to be in sympathy with the extreme zealots, and there was a trend in public opinion—as far as it was allowed to exist—which was taking a Puritan direction. In addition, as we have seen, there were other reasons which encouraged the Puritan section, and Puritanism came into the open with the results which have been considered in the last chapter. On the other hand, early legislation and the erection of a Protestant form of worship immediately placed Catholicism under the ban. Whatever else the

official policy might stand for, or be interpreted
to stand for, it was clear that it was uncompromis-
ingly opposed to the Catholic Church.   The
Elizabethan Church of 1559 owed its very origin
to the rejection of the Faith.   The earliest dealings
were aimed at Catholic bishops and clergy.   The
Puritan had reasons for hope, the Catholic none.
The Acts of Supremacy and Uniformity were, it is
true, aimed at any type of nonconformity, but they
would hardly have been passed had there been no
Catholicism.   However the government may have
intended to unravel religious problems as they
arose, one policy was certain to carry every class
of Protestant with it, and that was an unbending
attitude towards the Catholic Church.   Amid all
the internal disputes between Established Churchman and Puritan, one common feature emerges, that
the Catholic had neither part nor parcel in the inheritance.   Thus from the very beginning Catholicism was the definitely proscribed religion, and as
a consequence it is harder to trace its place in
parish life.   Puritanism could hope for anything
from a Government which had cast the Pope un-
ceremoniously out of England.   As the Puritan
held in his hand the New Service Book, and remembered that it owed its origin to Edwardine
extremes, and as he surveyed a bench of new
bishops almost entirely in sympathy with his theological position, there were many reasons for him
to trust the future.   But the Catholic, as he saw
the Queen appointed Supreme Governor of the
Church, and his worship inhibited in spite of the
unanimous opposition of his official representatives,

could only look out into the unknown region, convinced that he was an outcast and a religious pariah. Puritanism placed its challenge before the nation and took up the position which we have already surveyed. It was comparatively easy to see its influence in parochial life, as it sought publicity and had many reasons to think that it would be successful by a public campaign. Catholicism on the other hand saw, humanly speaking, no future in front of it, and its history lies largely in the secret places of parochial life. It is therefore a difficult work to follow it throughout the reign. The books of Catholic controversy, the acts of Catholic martyrs, the public prosecutions of Catholics, and the lists of Catholic exiles, help us very little when we come to consider Catholicism in parish life. In addition we have seen how the Government dealt with Catholic worship. Not only was it a penal offence, but the ornaments necessary for it had been ruthlessly destroyed. This chapter, then, must of necessity be very incomplete, as the documents of a secret religion are never likely to be numerous. However, we can rely on two sources of evidence: negative, from penal statutes and proclamations against Catholicism, which imply its existence in the country; and positive, from the various reports of bishops to the Government on the conditions of their dioceses, from episcopal orders enforced in the parishes, and from such Catholic documents as we possess. We shall deal in broad terms, leaving some smaller but important details for another chapter.

The history of Elizabethan Catholicism can be divided into five periods, each characterized by some outstanding event: the early dealings, gathering round the establishment of the new régime; those gathering round the accession of Pius IV, and culminating in the panic of 1563; the Northern rebellion; the fears before and after the Spanish Armada, and the concluding years of the reign. We shall deal, so far as space will allow, with Catholics in parochial life from the sources of evidence mentioned, under these five divisions. We shall doubtless be compelled to omit many facts which the reader might expect to find in this chapter. Details of history applying to a set of parishes, or to a few individuals, belong, however, to a complete history of the subject, and they can have no place in an attempt to present a study true, so far as possible, to parish life. Nor can any discussion of such questions as legality and treason come within the scope of such a study. We are here merely concerned with the facts—to take parish life as we find it, and to present it as it was.

The process of the Royal Visitation [1] of 1559 affords us very little evidence for our purpose, as we are not dealing with the Catholic clergy. Certain facts emerge, however, which are valuable when considered in connexion with what has already been said concerning this visitation. After the official Commissioners had presented the conditions already referred to, we find that in certain districts in Yorkshire the churchwardens reported

[1] The records of the Northern visitation are chiefly in *State Papers Domestic*, x.

that church attendance was neglected, and that in many parishes images still stood, or had been taken away and hidden, hoping for a time when they could be set up again. This fact was specially noted in parts of the diocese of Chester, where " papists " were reported by the local officials for hiding church property—especially service books. The Spanish Ambassador noted that, at this point, many were frightened by the constancy and number of Catholics in London, and that in Hampshire the New Service Book was most unpopular. He also wrote of reported disturbances from the parishes in the North on account of the new religion.[1] His predecessor had already informed his government that Catholics were in great majority in the country districts.[2] In the beginning of 1560 there were Masses in London. In addition, the history of the clerical deprivations shows—no matter what estimate we accept—that many of the deprived priests were able to obtain hiding places, " lurking among papists." Acting as private schoolmasters, or, risking detection, they earned a precarious living as common workmen, and carried out their ministrations among the faithful. The fact that official papers speak so often of them justifies us in concluding that their continued presence meant that a number of people remained Catholics. It must, however, be said that there is not much to be gained for our study from records or reports connected with this Visitation. When it broadened out, as it were, into the Metro-

[1] *Chron. Belg.*, 356. i. 540, 359. i. 544, 362. i. 548.
[2] *Ibid.*, 346. i. 518.

political Visitation of 1560 and 1561, we are able to add some more important facts. As far as possible we shall consider this Visitation according to dioceses. In the province of Canterbury—that is, in all the parishes south of Hull and Chester— Parker issued enquiries not merely as to whether the ornaments of Catholic worship had been destroyed, but whether any priests lurked in the various counties, and whether any divine service was celebrated other than that provided in the New Service Book. Orders were issued forbidding any one to favour a foreign power, or to speak against the religion now established.[1] In Winchester " the Common Prayer was not frequented since the Mass time and the people were opposed to good and sound doctrine." Sermons against the Pope and the Mass were necessary. Clergy hid with the nobility and gentry. When the bishop began severe dealings in one parish, Catholics moved off somewhere else. He demanded from the Government good sound preachers, as otherwise the diocese would continue in its " superstition and popery." The priests of the Cathedral were so " stubborn " that they would " inculcate into the heads of the people " their religion, and this would hinder him from reforming the country parishes, where many had not communicated " since the Mass-saying." In spite of all this zeal there were still in the diocese at the end of 1563 " errors circulated by the papists in secret."[2] The diocese of Hereford[3]

[1] *Parker MS. Register,* i. f. 302 (4, 13, 18).
[2] *State Papers Domestic*, xvii. 23, xix. 36, xxi. 7, *Zurich Letters*, i. No. 61.
[3] *Ibid.*, xix. 24, *Camden Miscellany*, ix. pp. 11 ff.

was in a state approaching anarchy. The cathedral church was " a very nursery of ignorance and superstition." Popish justices hindered reform in the parishes, and the butchers refused to sell meat on Thursdays. The Vigil and Feast of the Assumption were kept as holidays, and even the " poor gospellers " dare not work. Old fasts and feasts were still observed. The local justices escorted deprived priests through the streets " with torchlights . . . they could not much more reverently have entertained Christ himself." Attempts at arrest were fruitless. The bishop was "abhorred of the most part for religion," and among " the worshipful of the shire there (were) not many favourers of the true religion." Indeed, things went from bad to worse. In 1564, there were over fifty popish magistrates, and the city council of Hereford were to a man against the new religion. In the neighbouring county of Radnor not a justice could be relied on; some of them openly " prayed on popish primers " and their wives and families " used beads, being mortal enemies to true religion." Many had Masses in their houses and refused to come to church at all. Many never received Communion since the beginning of the reign, and kept in their homes " schools of Popery." False popish books were " magnified and extolled to the skies." In Bath and Wells certain justices were reported as " enemies to God's truth and the Queen's most godly proceedings," and the people were stubborn or temporizers.[1] Norwich presented violent extremes between Puri-

[1] *State Papers Domestic*, xvi. 27.

tanism and Catholicism. In some parishes the clergy and people maintained their popish altars and the details of Catholic ceremonial. Images still stood with pictures of the Assumption and the Annunciation. Holy-water stocks and old service-books were not uncommon. Not a few of the magistrates were papists, and refused to advance the new religion.[1] In the diocese of St. Asaph,[2] it was necessary to order the destruction of altars and relics, to reform church attendance, and to bring authority to bear on misbehaviour at public worship. In Ely there was widespread support given to the old religion. In many churches Catholic ornaments still remained intact in spite of injunctions, and the roods were often undefaced. The people were not anxious to conform to the new conditions. Few churches would purchase the *Book of Homilies*, many did not possess even the Prayer Book and Bible. Communion vessels as ordered were frequently wanting, and the general lack of preaching and services told its own tale of nonconformity.[3] More than two-thirds of the parishes lay vacant, or unprovided for.[4] There were an immense number of papists " for the most part lying concealed . . . cherishing their errors in secret assemblies."[5] In Salisbury,[6] Bishop Jewel found great obstinacy among

---

[1] *Ritual Report*, Appendix E. (1). *Camden Miscellany*, ix. pp. 47 ff.

[2] Wilkins, *Concilia*, iv. 228 (6-10).

[3] *Visitation MSS.* Ely (1561).

[4] *Additional MSS.* (Brit. Mus.) 5813, 78, cf. *Corpus Christi MSS. Cambridge*, cxxii.

[5] *Zurich Letters*, i. No. 49.

[6] Jewel, *Letters*, xxxiii.

the papists, and there was much disturbance caused
by their lurking in " hiding places and in corners."
In Chichester,[1] Barlow feared that secret, popish-
minded men might break out and disturb the peace
of his parishes at any time.   In London, the old
Rogation-tide processions were approved by many
people joining in them.[2]   Ecclesiastical punish-
ments seemed to be of no use to put down the Mass,
and many Catholics attended it.[3]   When we turn
to the Northern dioceses we have little reliable
information for this division of our subject, as
many of the bishoprics there were not filled at
once.   However, it is possible to arrive at some
idea of parochial Catholicism from miscellaneous
documents. Early in 1560 the diocese of Durham[4]
was " vastly out of order in matters of religion."
In the following year the Bishop compared his
efforts to enforce conformity to St. Paul struggling
with beasts at Ephesus.   The people were a " fro-
ward generation," and he did not know which of
them hated one another most.   The justices were
a source of trouble, and their refusal of godly religion encouraged parochial anarchy.   In Carlisle[5]
Mass was openly celebrated, and the Bishop was
afraid to proceed on his own initiative lest he
should fan the flame of Catholic ardour.   Books in
French encouraged the papists, who spoke openly
of a return to the old religion.   The magistrates

---

[1] *Camden Miscellany*, ix. 8.
[2] Strype, *Grindal*, 56, Grindal, *Remains*, 240.
[3] *State Papers Domestic*, xvi. 49.
[4] *Hatfield Papers*, 222, *State Papers Domestic*, **xx.**
5, 25.
[5] *Ibid.*, xviii. 21, xxi. 13.

" winked and looked through their fingers." In the large diocese of York,[1] there was a similar state of affairs. The justices had never heard of the Oath of Supremacy—so they alleged, and some of the nobility gave such encouragement to papists that the Bishop dare not visit his diocese. Leaving the evidence provided by such official documents as those referred to, some information for these years can be gained from other sources, such as letters and foreign correspondence. Thus, for example, we learn that in the early months of the reign a Catholic procession was carried out at Canterbury, when many people took part in it[2]; and " the opposition of papists " was sufficiently wide to be reported to Reformers on the continent. Many such letters could be quoted, but to do so would not give us much wider information, although it would go to prove that certainly during this period there was much " heart-searching " on account of " maintainers of error and superstition." In addition, when we consider later[3] the efforts made to enforce conformity during these years, it will become clearer that there must have been many Catholics who did not attend public worship, as the injunctions in this connexion can hardly apply to Puritanism, which, as we have seen, did not threaten the Elizabethan Settlement till a later date. Indeed evidence is not wanting—and that of a positive kind—that there was sufficient Catholicism left to warrant careful measures by the Government. Cecil's notes[4] furnish us with lists of Catholics

[1] *Ibid.*, xxi. 27.
[2] *Venetian Papers* (30 May, 1559).
[3] See below, chapter viii.
[4] *State Papers Domestic*, xvi. 14.

H

who required such attentions, and we know that Bishop Grindal[1] examined Catholic prisoners at this period, and that he learned from them that Mass was being celebrated in several parts of the country, and that the materials for Catholic worship were hidden in different places. We are not so much concerned with the actual treatment which prisoners received at this time, as with the fact that the names of such prisoners survive, and it is significant that opposite certain names Cecil wrote the word " Mass " and that his list is headed " Names of prisoners for the Mass."[2] It is reasonable to conclude that the celebration of Mass meant that there were many Catholics who sought Catholic worship. Broadly speaking then, it would seem that in many places the Reformation, during the years at present under review, did not call forth the allegiance which is commonly claimed for it. Sufficient evidence has been given to prove that many dioceses were, to use a contemporary phrase, " ill-disposed to the Queen's godly proceedings."

Before entering on the second division of this survey, it becomes necessary to recall certain events which in a greater or lesser degree bear upon it. Pius IV became Pope early after Queen Elizabeth's accession, and he at once proceeded to invite the Queen to return to the Catholic Church.[5] This invitation was entrusted to Parpaglia, Abbot of San Salvatore, Turin. The Queen acted in a characteristic manner. She professed to be highly pleased

---

[1] *Ibid.*, xvi. 49.   [2] *Ibid.*, Ad., xi. 8.
[8] Cardwell, *Documentary Annals*, I. li. and compare W. P. M. Kennedy, *Parker*, pp. 146 ff.

with the business, said Catholicism was only under a temporary shadow, and that the papal envoy would be welcome. The hopes of Catholics at home revived, and with them those of the Catholic exiles in France, who received the envoy on his arrival there with joy. But Parpaglia never entered England. Elizabeth was merely playing a game, and he returned to Rome in high disgust over his treatment. It was easy for her to make the excuse that Parpaglia was a Frenchman and that, if she admitted him to England, Philip of Spain would not approve. As in most religious affairs in the reign, political considerations held the upper place. The Spanish monarch's friendship, and a determination to provide no rallying place in England for Catholics, were of much greater moment to the Queen than courteous letters about religion, which was never under any form real to her. The Savoyard ambassador to Scotland also failed to move her on his way to the Scottish court. Early in 1561 another papal envoy, Martinengo, arrived in Flanders bearing an invitation to the Council of Trent. Once more the political side came to the front. The Council discussed the question of admitting him, and decided that his presence in the country would be dangerous to domestic peace. It was clear, in addition, that England could only be represented by sending a deprived prelate. Elizabeth's enthusiasm waned when she saw that her own bishops could take no part in the Council. However, at one time she wished to receive him, and even proposed that the Spanish Ambassador and Archbishop Parker should discuss the matter.

The latter astutely refused, saying that " it would
be construed among the light brethren in divers
respects."[1]   In this he was no doubt correct, for
the Spanish Ambassador was the acknowledged
leader of the English Catholics, and in this
capacity he obtained a decision from the Pope on
the question of the English Service.   Many
Catholics had deceived themselves that there was
no harm in going to Morning or Evening Prayer in
the Protestant Church, as this consisted merely of
collects, psalms, and Scripture. They thought that
such services might be open to them, so long as
they were not present at the Holy Communion. The
Spanish Ambassador on 7 Aug. 1562, sent a set of
questions about the matter to Rome prefaced by
the following remarks:[2] " The case is novel and
unusual; it is very different from an ordinary case
of communicating with excommunicants.   The
question *Si est metus aut coactio* cannot be seriously
raised; the coercion is absolute, for capital punishment is imposed on everyone who will not live as a
heretic.   Also in this instance we have only to do
with presence at what are called ' Common
Prayers,' and these contain no impiety or false
doctrine, for they consist of Scriptures and prayers
taken from the Catholic Church, though what concerns the merits and intercession of Saints has been
omitted.   Moreover, we have not to deal with the
Communion, which is celebrated only at Easter and
other great festivals.   The question is solely as to
presence at their Common Prayers."   Pius IV re-

---

[1] *Parker Correspondence*, No. cliii.
[2] F. W. Maitland, *Collected Papers*, iii. 178.

turned an emphatically negative answer—presence
at no form of Protestant worship could be allowed.
It is interesting to note that this answer was returned in spite of three considerations. First, the
Spanish Ambassador clearly hoped for an affirma-
tive reply.   Second, he exaggerated the punishment and omitted to mention that reception of the
Lord's Supper was enforced three times a year at
least by the Prayer Book; and third, many
Catholics had conformed to Common Prayers. This
third consideration led to authority being granted
to the Spanish Ambassador, and to others through
him, to grant absolution to those who had resorted
to such worship.   Whatever Catholics may have
been led to believe or hope through the various
reports circulated during the negotiations over
Trent, it was made clear to them that Pius IV
would grant no concessions, and action on the part
of the Government soon proved that the official
attitude towards Catholicism was as uncompromising as ever. A new Ecclesiastical Commission[1] was
drawn up in July, 1562, which contained some
significant powers. For example, the Commissioners were ordered to search out nonconformists,
to furnish fines into the Exchequer for nonconformity, and to enquire after all heresies and sedi-
tious books.   The result of this new Commission
was at once apparent. We have a new list[2] of
Catholics drawn up a few weeks later. This list
contains the names of clerical and lay Catholic nonconformists.   In connexion with the latter, certain

[1] *State Papers Domestic*, xxvi. 41.
[2] *Ibid*., Ad., xi. 45.

facts emerge which are noteworthy in relation to
our study. We find that two schoolmasters and
several university students have been put under
restraint, that four gentlemen are in prison; and
that the greater part of the counties of Stafford
and Derby " are generally evil-inclined towards
religion and forbear coming to church and parti-
cipating in the Sacraments " because Catholic
gentlemen had been imprisoned.   In addition
Elizabeth took the side of the French Huguenots
and sent soldiers to their aid.   Catholics, if they
went to church, were compelled to listen to prayers
for these soldiers "who went over the seas to the aid
of such as be persecuted for Thy Holy Name, and
to withstand the cruelty of those which be common
enemies as well to the truth of Thy eternal word
as to their own natural prince and countrymen and
manifestly to this Crown and realm of England."[1]
Parliament in 1563 crowned the national panic by
a Penal Act.[2]   Those who maintained the power
and jurisdiction of the Pope by " writing, preaching, teaching, open act or deed " and their abettors,
were pronounced guilty of *praemunire* for the first
offence, and of high treason for the second. Similar
penalties extended to those who should refuse the
Oath of Supremacy.   This general history has been
necessary at this point as it all provides negative
evidence of the existence of Catholicism up and
down the country.   It must be specially noted that
the Spanish Ambassador's appeal to Rome, a new
and severe Ecclesiastical Commission, and a severe

---

[1] *Liturgical Services* . . . *Queen Elizabeth*, p. 476.
[2] 5 Eliz., c. i.

Penal Act were hardly the outcome of isolated cases of Catholic nonconformity. The Spanish Ambassador wrote, as he said, " for the Catholics of this realm," and the previous legislation would have been sufficiently strong to stamp out isolated Catholics. Nor must this evidence be considered apart from the survey which we shall make later of the enforcing of the Act of Uniformity. Negatively, we are able to conclude that Catholicism was still strong in the parishes. We now turn to positive evidence up to the accession of Pius V, in 1566. As before, we shall group it under diocesan reports as far as possible. In the province of Canterbury enquiries were made in 1563 regarding the survival of Catholic ornaments, whether Mass was said or heard in private, and whether there were any favourers of the Bishop of Rome.[1] In Winchester Bishop Horne was engaged in attempting to make the congregation in the Cathedral behave decently, and in demanding throughout the diocese signatures to a form of declaration based on the Penal Acts, and declaring that the Elizabethan Settlement was " according to the true Word of God and agreeing with the doctrine and use of the primitive and apostolic Church."[2] He informed Bullinger that he was doing his utmost to counteract " the errors which are circulated by the Papists in secret,"[3] and he found, as he told Cecil, that in Hampshire and Surrey there were not a few favourers of Papistry

---

[1] *Second Ritual Report*, App. E., p. 403.
[2] *Horne MS. Register*, ff. 12, 14v, 15, 15v.
[3] *Zurich Letters*, i. 61.

among the justices, while in the City of Winchester
" all that (bore) authority except one or two (were)
addicted to the old superstition and earnest
favourers thereof."[1]   In the diocese of Hereford,
out of one hundred and twenty-three magistrates
reported on, fifty-four were found to be in
sympathy with Catholicism, and conditions had not
improved since the early years of the reign.[2]   In
Norwich there were a few " not well bent " to the
new religion.[3]   In December, 1563, Bishop Cox
of Ely informed the Government that " Papists
swarmed in all corners saying and doing almost
what they list " and that books of Catholic controversy were flying " abroad in all corners."[4]   In
Salisbury many " hinderers of religion " were
found among the magistrates, and, among the
gentry characterized as such, appears the name of
the great Elizabethan lawyer Edmund Plowden.
There were still " some popish satellites " who
made as much disturbance as they could in
" corners and secret places."[5] In London many continued to hear Mass at the houses of the foreign ambassadors,[6] and many received absolution and the
Sacraments. In the diocese of Rochester the Bishop
issued inquiries for those who frequented or celebrated Mass, and for favourers of Romish power,
and ordered that old holydays which had been

---

[1] *Harleian MSS.* (Brit. Mus.), 595. 31. f. 258.
[2] See above p. 93.
[3] *Camden Miscellany*, ix. pp. 47 ff.
[4] *Lansdowne MSS.*, vi. 87.
[5] *Camden Miscellany*, ix. pp. 37 ff.   Jewel, *Letters*,
xxxvii.
[6] *Simancas State Papers*, 223, *Cotton MSS.*, Gab. c. i.
29.

abrogated should not be kept.[1]   In Coventry and
Lichfield the entire county " was hinderly in all
good things pertaining to religion " and " divers
lewd priests " encouraged the people, and the
magistrates were sufficiently " unreformed " to
prevent Protestant progress.[2]   In many places
service books and the ornaments of Catholic worship, with Catholic burial customs, still survived.
In Peterborough the Bishop found " straggling
doctors and priests " who did " much hurt to religion," and he asked the Government to compel
them to make " an open recantation."   He also
complained that there were many Catholic schoolmasters in Catholic houses, who did " great hurt
in the country round about them."[3]   In Worcester
the Bishop pleaded for the appointment of Protestant magistrates and for severe measures against
" popish and perverse priests " who " perverted the
simple and blasphemed the truth."[4] Of the diocese
of Bangor Cecil was informed that " there were
many dregs of superstition . . . images and altars
stood in the churches undefaced . . . lewd and indecent vigils and watches were observed ; much
pilgrimage going ; many candles set up in honour
of the Saints ; some relics yet carried about and
all the counties full of beads and knots, besides
divers other monuments of wilful serving of
God."[5]   When we turn to the Northern province

---

[1] *Rochester MSS.*, vii. f. 98 (5, 7), f. 98v (10).
[2] *Camden Miscellany*, ix. pp. 39 ff.; *State Papers Domestic*, xxxvi. 41 (5, 21).
[3] *Camden Miscellany*, ix. pp. 34 ff.
[4] *Ibid.*, pp. 1. ff.
[5] *State Papers Domestic*, xliv. 27.

the documentary evidence is much less wide. The
City of Durham was far from satisfactory, being
reported as "very stiff," while in parts of
Lancashire Protestantism seemed to make little
progress.[1]   A special Ecclesiastical Commission
was appointed in 1562 for Chester, but in spite of
its work the whole diocese was out of hand, as
was alleged, through the Bishop's negligence.[2]   In
York there was much murmuring and trifling with
true religion, and throughout the North generally,
the magistrates could not be trusted.

When Pius V became Pope in January, 1566, it
was at once clear that a new era had dawned for
English Catholics.[3]   The days for delay and hope
were over, and the first agent of the new policy
was sent to England in the person of Lawrence
Vaux, with powers to reconcile those who had un-
wittingly taken part in heresy.   This mission marks
a distinct point in the study of Catholicism.   We
shall find wider evidences of repression, as the
"true papist" takes the place of the "secret or
cunning papist."   Events moved rapidly, and on
August 14, 1567, a formal Bull of Reconciliation
was issued, with a solemn form of absolution
attached.   In the following January official enquiries were begun in the various dioceses for
Catholics, and in May the arrival of Mary Queen
of Scots in England served not only to complicate

[1] *Lansdowne MSS.*, vii. 12;   *Parker Correspondence*,
No. clxviii.

[2] *State Papers Domestic*, xxiii. 56.

[3] Materials for the later history must be sought in
Sharpe, *Memorials of Northern Rebellion; Depositions and
Ecclesiastical Proceedings* (Surtees Society);   *York Arch.
Journal*, xviii.

the position of Catholics, but to provide a rallying-point for their political hopes. The first act under the new conditions took place in Lancashire, where the gentry had organized themselves into a body bound by oath not to conform nor receive the Holy Communion during the Queen's reign. In Yorkshire, leaders from abroad appeared, furnished with the ways and means of rebellion. Plot and counter-plot characterized the following year, and finally the North broke into open revolt in the early winter of 1569. In three months every hope from armed resistance had vanished, and executions and heavy fines closed the scene. Pius V excommunicated Elizabeth, and Parliament replied with severe measures. It was enacted that those who brought in bulls or absolutions should be guilty of high treason—abettors were made liable to *praemunire*, as well as those who imported into the country crosses, beads, pictures, and such like objects of Catholic piety. We are not concerned with this rebellion in its political aspect, and that side of its history must be read elsewhere. We shall see, however, that the general history of these years provides us with some valuable material for estimating the strength of Catholicism. This strength, it is true, never was coherent, and Catholics were too carefully watched to give them any hope of success in organized revolt; but that there was a strong Catholic element throughout the country will be clear after examination of the evidence. We shall continue to follow the diocesan documents and reports. For the province of Canterbury[1] —

---

[1] *Canterbury Visitations*, Brit. Museum, T. 775 (9) (1573); *Parker MS. Register*, i. 320 (1569); Cardwell, *Annals*, i. 337 (1567).

that is for two-thirds of England—we have archiepiscopal orders for the years 1567, 1569 and 1573. These provide proof that nonconformists, favourers of "Romish power," and users of "superstitious beads" existed in different places in the parishes covered by these injunctions. In Norwich, Catholic customs commonly survived, images still stood undemolished, and unlicensed schoolmasters taught in 1569.[1] In Winchester private Masses, Catholic customs at Rogation-tide, and monuments of idolatry were found in 1575.[2] A few years previously the Bishop complained that the people generally hoped that the Queen would soon "alter this religion" and there were high expectations among the Papists. Lists of Recusants were soon drawn up for this diocese.[3] In Worcester the books of Catholic exiles were in circulation in 1569, Mass was said in corners, efforts were made "to seduce the simple people," books of Catholic devotion survived, and "the usurped authority of the Bishop of Rome and other points of popery" were maintained. In the same year the Bishop informed Cecil of the state of his diocese, and Cecil endorsed the letters "papists or favourers in those parts."[4] In 1571 Bishop Cox enforced conformity in the diocese of Ely.[5] He found many papists abroad "who were a stumbling block to the godly," who resorted to secret Masses.

[1] *Second Ritual Report*, App. E., p. 404.
[2] *Winchester Visitation*, Brit. Museum, 5155. de. 24 (7, 22).
[3] *Lansdowne MSS.*, xii. 31; *State Papers Domestic*, xc. 18; cxvii. 10; cxlii. 33.
[4] *Lansdowne MSS.*, xi. f. 204 (26, 30, 32, 35).
[5] *Second Ritual Report*, App. E., p. 406.

Efforts to compel them to come to church were frequently productive of mere change of abode.[1] In the diocese of Rochester (during the years 1571-1574), popish gear was reserved in private houses; popish prayer books were used; people ran from place to place "under pretence of an hypocritical Romish conscience"; "papists, idolators, invokers of Saints departed, defenders of false doctrines, men's merits, holy water, holy bread and of Romish pardon" were abroad.[2] It is only possible to glance at the state of London, where Mass at the residences of the foreign ambassadors encouraged Catholics. Indeed Catholicism assumed such proportions in the capital that Archbishop Parker began enquiries among the lawyers, as the various Inns seemed to be the chief centres of lay-Catholics. He soon found that many were suspected of "hearing Mass, Mattins and Evensong in Latin, and of being shriven and houseled after the popish manner."[3] It is interesting to note that during the reign Catholicism was strong among the lawyers, and that some of the most brilliant members of the Elizabethan bar supported the old religion. In connexion with the North, the evidence of Catholicism is too wide to be noted in such elaborate detail. One reference will suffice as it covers all the parishes north of Hull and Chester. Bishop Grindal found it necessary to forbid the clergy giving Communion into the mouths

[1] *Zurich Letters*, i. 88; *State Papers Domestic*, cxvii. 28.

[2] *Rochester MSS.*, vii. f. 118 (2) f. 128v (14, 19).

[3] *State Papers Domestic*, xlviii. 26; lx. 70; *Petyt MSS.*, 538. 47. f. 342; *Parker Correspondence*, ccxc. 1.

of the people as used heretofore; breathing on the bread and showing it to the congregation to be worshipped and adored; observing Catholic fasts and holy days and enjoining their observation. The churchwardens were ordered to destroy the Roods and images, and to abolish utterly all books of the Latin service. Purgatory and prayers for the dead were denounced as superstitions. The people were commanded not to go " to popish priests for shrift or auricular confession in Lent or at any other time," and returns were asked of those who favoured the Romish religion, or who heard or said Mass. Grindal's orders belong to the year 1571.[1] If we did not know the date, a cursory glance through them would almost convince us that they belonged to the beginning of the reign. Catholic customs were widespread all over the Northern parishes. Mass was celebrated; priests lurked among the people. From the evidence which has been produced it is clear that up to 1580 there was no inconsiderable number of Catholics in England. The persecutions and martyrdoms lie outside our survey; but if we were to add the negative evidence drawn from the missionary efforts of such men as Mayne, Nelson and Sherwood, we should be forced to conclude that Catholicism was a serious element in parochial life.

It would take us too far afield to consider the later history of Elizabethan Catholicism[2] in such

---

[1] *Second Ritual Report*, App. E., pp. 411 ff.

[2] For the later history of Elizabethan Catholicism see *Records of the English Catholics*; Challoner, *Memoirs*; *State Papers Domestic*, cxviii. 46, 47; Simpson, *Life of Campion*.

close detail as has been attempted up to the arrival
of the first Jesuit missionaries in the spring of
1580. The work of Campion and Persons hardly
needs elaboration, but the Government had such
a reply ready to their devotion as goes almost
further than anything else to prove the scattered
strength of Catholicism. A new penal law was
passed in 1581, which condemned "massing" to
fines and imprisonment, and absence from church
to the enormous fine of £20 per month. England
now became a huge religious hunt-meeting, and
as may be expected, after years of careful training,
the hounds were always close on the quarry. Before the end of 1583, 124 clergy, and 53 men and
women of the laity were done to death according
to the brutal methods of the age. But repression
did not damp missionary work. In the South of
England, along the Welsh Border and in the North,
the people clung to the Catholic Faith, and extended a generous welcome to those who came to
their aid in spiritual matters. We are not concerned to discuss the political aspect of Catholicism,
which at this point certainly came to the front, and
did more than anything else to make the persecutions severer and more continuous. Even if we
discount the estimate for the sake of argument by
deducting politically-minded Catholics, there still
remains evidence that there was a considerable
number of Catholics in the country who were prepared to suffer for religion and who did suffer for
religion. Beyond that, space and the nature of
our study forbid us to go. The official dealings
varied under the rise or fall of public panic. Thus

in 1585,[1] all priests ordained out of England since June 24th of the previous year were ordered to leave the country, and those who received them were liable to punishment as felons. No child could be educated abroad without special licence. On the other hand, plots gathered round Mary Queen of Scots, and her execution in 1587 was only a part of panic action. The coming and the failure of the Spanish Armada left marks on Catholic history. A new Penal Act was passed in 1593.[2] Catholics in future were to be confined within an area of five miles from their homes, and were banished if they transgressed this regulation. Fines and restraint paid the Government better than banishments. Fears of a new Spanish fleet brought further repression. The prisons were filled, and lists of seven hundred Catholics in Lancashire, two hundred in Cheshire, and three hundred in Hampshire were presented to the Government. These Hampshire Catholics were thrown into prison at Farnham Castle and Banbury. Official dealings became so strong that the question once more arose of conformity by attendance at Morning Prayer, but once more the Pope decided that such a procedure was unlawful. Affairs moved from bad to worse, and although loyalty to the Throne was evident among Catholics, yet they suffered from the political methods indulged in by their fellow-Catholics abroad, who seemed in these concluding years to have misjudged the position in England and to have acted in such a way

[1] 27 Eliz., c. ii.   [2] 35 Eliz., c. ii.

as neither hope of political success nor consideration for their brethren would warrant. There can
be little doubt that the unedifying disputes which
arose between missionaries trained abroad and the
secular priests working in England might have
been averted. The Government played one party
off against the other and then issued a proclamation
against toleration of any kind, spite of solemn professions of loyalty with which the reign closes.
A cursory reference to documents must suffice to
illustrate something of the history of these years.
Their history has occupied the attention of many
modern writers, and need not be elaborated here.
Thus in 1583, many of the people of Winchester
diocese openly declared that they hoped to have the
Mass again soon.[1] In Coventry and Lichfield in
the following year, search was made for massing
priests, and for priests who went about as laymen,
and encouraged among the people support for the
" Romish Church."[2] In Norwich in the same year
Mass was celebrated in the city and some of the
Bishop's household were present.[3] In 1582, 327
Catholic families were known to the Government
in Yorkshire, and in Lancashire the return was
made at 428.[4] In Chichester diocese the people
resorted to Mass and to popish priests for shrift
in 1585.[5] In the following year a general proclamation for the entire country was issued against
popish books.[6] In the diocese of Salisbury in 1588

[1] *Cotton MSS.*, Tit. B. 29. f. 73.
[2] *Second Ritual Report*, App. E., p. 428.
[3] *Lansdowne MSS.*, xl. 14.
[4] *Dictionary of National Biography*, xii. 150.
[5] *Whitgift MS. Register*, i. f. 116 (vii.).
[6] Strype, *Whitgift*, i. 513.

I

there is evidence that reconciliations to the Church
were taking place.[1]   In 1595 a letter from the
Council was sent through Archbishop Whitgift to
every diocese in England, ordering the bishops to
furnish lists of recusants—men, women, children
and servants—and this command was carried out
by the parish clergy in the parishes of the land.
It would be wearisome to give further details which
are forthcoming from similar diocesan documents[2]
for Ely, Lincoln, Exeter, London, Hereford and
Bristol down to the end of the reign.   The State
Papers abound in evidence.

We are now in a position to examine Dr.
Creighton's statement: " In England generally the
religious settlement was welcomed by the people
and corresponded to their wishes."[3]   As we sum-
marize the impression made by the documents
which we have examined, it must be clear that such
a judgment is not established by facts.   From the
days of the Royal Visitation down to the last
Visitation of the reign—from the earliest episcopal
letters to the Government down to the final collections of State Papers, there is more than abundant
evidence to prove that Elizabethan Catholicism
must not be judged by the records of executions,

[1] *Whitgift MS. Register*, i. f. 400.
[2] Ely, 1597 (*Whitgift Register*, iii. 164).   Lincoln, 1598
(Brit. Mus. 5155. a. 20 (5)).   Exeter, 1599 (*Ibid.*, 5155. a. 19).
London, 1601 (*Ritual Report*, p. 436).   Hereford, 1602 (Brit.
Mus. 5155. aa. 20).   Bristol, 1603 (*Ritual Report*, p. 440).
[3] *Queen Elizabeth*, p. 53 (1912).   Mrs. Creighton has
modified Dr. Creighton's estimate of the number of nonconforming priests by a reference to Dom Birt's book,
but no modification has taken place with regard to the
laity.

by lists of fines, or by names returned to the Government. These indeed provide their own quota of weight, but there can be no doubt that in almost every diocese, parochial Catholicism was something more than a family here and there. Nor will national panics explain the documents. On all sides we must confess that Catholicism had to be reckoned with. When the inner history of the various sufferers for the Faith who were mixed up with politics is added to what has been written here, it must be beyond cavil that the religious settlement was not generally welcomed by the people. The next chapter will serve from another point of view to emphasize this conclusion. As a modern historian[1] has said, " at the end of her reign perhaps Elizabeth flattered herself that she was within measurable distance of religious uniformity." History confirms that it was only " flattery."

CHAPTER VIII.

ENFORCING THE IDEAL.

UP to this point we have surveyed the new system as erected by Queen Elizabeth in its origin and in its relation to the churches, clergy and services of the parishes. The rise of Puritanism and the attempt at its suppression as well as the slow process of crushing out Catholicism have also been

---

[1] E. S. Beesley, *Queen Elizabeth*, p. 229. Compare J. Hobson Matthews, *Cardiff Records*, ii. (1900). Mr. Matthews records that the county gaol was crowded with Catholics in 1598, and that in 1602 there were in the city alone, nineteen Catholic gentlemen who were obstinate in their refusal to conform.

considered. Through every chapter of our study there has emerged something of the process of forcing the Elizabethan ideal of religion on the parishes. We have seen Acts of Parliament with penalties applied to everyday life; clergy and laity dragooned to new positions; churches and services changed by drastic legislation, and the best and most conscientious people crushed, to a large degree, out of parochial life. The Government were not content to let the system worm its way into the hearts of the people by merely broad methods of gentle pressure. They determined that there should be deep, radical changes, and that anything which stood in the way of those changes should be firmly swept away. Half-measures had no place in the system, especially where Catholic traditions or practices were concerned. As a consequence there are some aspects of parochial life in this connexion which cannot be overlooked and without which even a broad survey such as we have attempted to make would not be true to life, and would lack certain important and indeed far-reaching elements. These aspects are private devotions and Catholic customs, parish officials, and education; and the Government endeavoured to control all three and to utilize them in enforcing their ideal.

Many practices of Catholic piety and many old Catholic customs lingered in the parishes of Elizabethan England, but few if any of them escaped the notice of the authorities, who feared that their survival would hinder the complete realization of the religious ideal aimed at. Bells continued to be rung on All Saints' Day and on All Souls' Day in honour of the Saints, and to remind the parishioners to pray specially for the Holy Dead of their own parish. Such a custom was completely at variance with the new religion, which had officially declared in Convocation in 1563 that " Doctrina Romanensium de purgatorio . . . nec non de invocatione sanctorum res est futilis, inaniter conficta." Unsuccessful efforts were made at the same Convocation[1] to prohibit such ringing; and it was uniformly forbidden by the bishops, especially in those parishes where the custom had gained a stronghold. In 1569, ringing on All Saints' Evening and on All Souls' Day was prohibited in Norfolk " as a superstitious ceremony used to the maintenance of popery or praying for the dead."[2] The custom died so slowly that the Southern Convocation of 1571 found it necessary to pass a canon against it,[3] and in the same year Archbishop Grindal was compelled to make gallant efforts to kill it, as it was almost universal in the parishes of all the Northern counties. He found that it " tended to maintain popish purgatory," and as a " gross superstition " must be abolished. He demanded the names of the ringers for censure and punishment.[4] Even instances of such ringing in London and the neigh-

---

[1] Strype, *Annals*, I. ii. App. A.
[2] *Ritual Report*, App. E., p. 405.
[3] *Canons of* 1571. (Church Historical Society, xl.). There is a manuscript copy of these canons in Corpus Christi Library, Cambridge (vol. cxxi. 34) signed not only by the southern Bishops, but by Abp. Grindal of York and the Bishops of Durham and Chester.
[4] *Second Ritual Report*, App. E., pp. 408, 411.

bourhood are extant, and " the superstition " was
maintained within the very hearing of the Government as late as 1572.[1] In connexion with bells
it may be well to note that in places the use of the
" sacring bell " lingered—especially in Staffordshire, Warwickshire, and the North. This may
have been due to the conformity of such priests
as Cardinal Allen mentioned,[2] but the Government
noted the fact and the bishops ordered the churchwardens to silence them.[3] Another custom which
died slowly was connected with Candlemas Day.
In Catholic times the people were accustomed to
bring candles to church, which were blessed and
carried in procession. In the middle of the reign
this custom still continued in the North of England
and was sternly put down " as burning candles
superstitiously."[4] Indeed the symbolism of lighted
candles was too strong a tradition to be easily
extirpated, and in not a few parishes lighted tapers
in the hands of godparents still glimmered round
the font of Baptism, until prohibited as a " popish
ceremony." But perhaps the custom which survived longest and caused the Government most
anxiety in this connexion was the use of Rosaries.
England's devotion to our Lady in Catholic times
was proverbial. In 1399, Archbishop Arundel
wrote:[5] " We English being the servants of her
special inheritance and her own dowry, as we are

---

[1] *London Articles* (1572), Brit. Mus. 698. h. 20 (10);
Freke MSS., No. viii. f. 128v.
[2] See above, p. 34.
[3] See for example, *State Papers Domestic*, xxxvi. 41
(21).
[4] *Second Ritual Report, op. cit.*
[5] Wilkins, *Concilia*, iii. 246.

commonly called, ought to surpass others in the
fervour of our devotion and praises." Every large
church had a chapel in her honour, and the smallest
parish church possessed a Lady altar.[1] Churches
dedicated to her studded the land, and " our gentle
Lady's Rosary" was one of the most universal
forms of devotion. As soon as the Reformation
gained the upper hand in England, an attack was
made on Rosaries. Cranmer strictly forbade their
use in 1548,[2] and the Homilies of 1547 condemned
them. Under Elizabeth, condemnation and pro-
hibition were renewed with such diligent persist-
ence that we are forced to conclude that a great
devotion to Mary lingered for many years among
the people. Indeed the evidence stretches over
the whole reign and refers to almost the whole
country. In East Anglia search was made in 1561
for " beads " and those who used them.[3] In
Northern Kent in 1565 the churchwardens were
asked to return the names of those who prayed " in
English or Latin upon beads."[4] In the parishes
of Derbyshire, Worcestershire and Shropshire the
clergy were ordered[5] in the same year " to call
upon the people daily that they cast away their
beads with all superstitions that they do use upon
them and to follow the right use of prayer . . .
which consisteth not in numbering their beads. . ."
Indeed these counties were so " notorious for bead-
using " that the bishop ordered the parish officials

[1] Bridgett, *Our Lady's Dowry*, 247.
[2] Cranmer, *Remains*, 154.
[3] *Brit. Mus. Articles*, 5155. aa. 8 (37, 58).
[4] *Guest MSS.*, vii. f. 98.
[5] *State Papers Domestic*, xxxvi. 41 (2).

to fine every one found with them " for every time
twelve pence to pay to the poor man's box."   In
1567 Parker found it necessary to send orders
against " beads " into every parish south of Hull
and Chester.¹   This order was repeated with a
request for defaulters in the parishes of Worcester
and Warwickshire in 1569.²   In 1571, all the
clergy and churchwardens of the Northern counties
were commanded to see that none of their parishioners used or possessed beads, and this pro-
hibition was accompanied by an injunction that
their people were to be forbidden " superstitiously
to make upon themselves the sign of the cross when
they first enter into any church to pray."³   Other
customs were ruthlessly crushed out.   Some
ventured to raise their voices in favour of the " holy
loaf " or of " holy water,"⁴ but the only satisfaction which they received were orders to receive
communion according to households " as they were
wont to pay the holy loaf "⁵ and to destroy all holy-
water stoups in their houses.⁶   We have already
referred to the search carried out in the homes of
the people for " old service books,"⁷ but this search
did not stop with them.   The people were abso-
lutely forbidden to use in public or private any
books of Catholic Devotions—" popish primers and
other like books "—or to keep in their houses any

¹ Cardwell, *Annals*, i. 337.
² *Lansdowne MSS.*, xi. f. 204 (29).
³ *Second Ritual Report*, App. E., *op. cit.* (41).
⁴ *Freke MSS.*, *op. cit.* (21).
⁵ *E g.*, *State Papers Domestic*, xxxvi. 41 (10).
⁶ *E.g.*, *Brit. Mus. Articles*, 698. h. 20 (10) [33].
⁷ See above, p. 50.

sacred pictures or images. Such books and objects of piety were demanded by the churchwardens in visiting the parishioners.[1] Finally the old Rogation Processions were brought into line. Processional crosses, banners and hand-bells lingered here and there, the clergy wearing surplices and stopping at the sites of old parochial crosses, and using " other like popish ceremonies."[2] These processions were turned into sombre " perambulations " with two Psalms, readings from Scripture, and a Homily, and only a few of the " substantial men in the parish " selected by the minister and churchwardens were allowed to " perambulate."[3]

These details may seem somewhat unnecessary, but they have been largely overlooked by Elizabethan historians. They illustrate the determination that no relic of Catholic times should be allowed to survive. In addition, they prove how severe were the regulations enforced to stamp out Catholic piety. Nothing escaped the vigilant eyes of the Government. The homes of the people were at the mercy of the churchwardens, who practically became Government spies, and even the possession of a Rosary or a sacred picture was considered a serious offence. Everywhere the Elizabethan ideal was forced on the people, and the minutest details of their piety were watched both in public and private and reported to the authorities. This official diligence characterized the entire reign, and this

[1] The evidence is drawn from the last four documents quoted.

[2] See Grindal, *Remains*, p. 204, and compare Strype, *Grindal*, p. 56.

[3] *Second Ritual Report, op. cit.* (43).

fact forces us to believe that, in many a parish, Catholic piety and traditions continued to linger long after England had been robbed of the Faith. It cannot be too strongly insisted on that the Government took up and developed a position far beyond that of mere conformity. At first there was a disposition to be satisfied with a general outward acceptance of the new régime, but as we have seen, the reign was not many years old before drastic measures were taken to deprive the people of Catholic traditions and of the objects and methods of Catholic piety. These measures were not confined to public worship nor outward parochial customs, but they entered into the private lives of the people, and nonconformity at home was as severely looked into in the Elizabethan religious dealings as a refusal to come to church and take part in Protestant public worship. This method of dealing with Catholics had however the advantage of being consistent. If the Puritan could not have his prayer-meeting and his " prophesyings " no more could the Catholic have his Rosary and his sacred pictures. If new secret Protestant worship was put down as antagonistic to the ideal, more so was private Catholic piety, because it tended to link the people with some of the oldest and most hallowed traditions of their race. Devotions intensified by future hopes, and devotions sanctified by centuries must be swept away if the avowed aim of the Elizabethan régime was to be realized. This aim may be summed up as the Established Church, the whole Established Church and nothing but the Established Church, and it is written large over the entire reign and in the smallest details of its religious life.

The frequent mention of churchwardens in this book will have helped to explain some of their duties. Indeed, *mutatis mutandis,* they continued the work of their Catholic predecessors. To this, however, were added other duties, such as administering poor-laws and carrying out certain sections of the Act of Uniformity. They ceased in many respects to be purely parish officials, and became in a very real sense officers of the Crown. It will now be necessary to consider them from this point of view. One of their most important new duties was to see that everyone in the parish attended the Parish Church. The Act of Uniformity ordered that a fine was to be imposed on any parishioner who was absent from church on Sundays and holy-days, and " that every person so offending shall forfeit for every such offence twelve pence, to be levied by the churchwardens of a parish where such offence shall be done, to the use of the poor of the same parish, of the goods, lands and tenements . . . by way of distress."[1] In addition such a misdemeanour was to be punished by ecclesiastical censure. The Royal Injunctions commanded the clergy to appoint " three or four discreet men " in each parish to superintend the attendance at church of the parishioners. They were to admonish offenders, and if they were still negligent to forward their names to the Ordinary.[2] These Injunctions made no mention of the statu-

[1] i Eliz., c. ii., 3.
[2] *Royal Injunctions of* 1559. No. 46.

tory fine, and if we may argue from lack of evidence, it would seem that the fine was not widely imposed until after the beginnings of Puritanism, and the Pope's refusal to permit attendance at the English service, already referred to.[1]   Indeed it must be confessed that many Catholics conformed outwardly even after attendance at Protestant worship was prohibited, and that it was not till Mary Queen of Scots arrived in England in 1568 that Catholic nonconformity became more common. However, there is evidence from 1561 onwards that the strict law was not a mere dead letter.   It will be well to examine this evidence in some detail, as there has been a disposition, especially among recent writers, to minimize this fact, and to state in broad terms that the fines were only imposed intermittently during the reign.   The extant documents prove that during the years 1561—1603, the churchwardens were uniformly compelled to attend to their legal duty in this respect.   We must examine these documents chronologically if we are to see how carefully the Government enforced the ideal.   In 1561 the united episcopate ordered that the churchwardens should hand in monthly lists to the parish clergyman, for the use of the bishops, of those " who will not readily pay their penalties for not coming to God's Divine Service according to the statutes."[2]   In 1563 all the churchwardens in the diocese of Canterbury were asked for returns " of what money had been

[1] See above, p. 100.
[2] Kennedy, *Interpretations of the Bishops*, pp. 31, 41.

gathered of the forfeits " for nonconformity.[1]   In
1565 we find that the general episcopal order of
1561 was enforced in the same terms in every
parish in the Middle-North of Kent.[2]   In the same
year the churchwardens of the parishes in Derbyshire and Staffordshire were commanded to punish
offenders " after one monition . . . according to
statute that is to pay twelve pence to the poor man's
box as often as they be absent."[3]   In 1566, the
general Episcopal Injunctions, known as " The
Advertisements," reinforced the earlier episcopal
order, for the whole of England.[4]   In 1569 we
find that the fines were imposed in many of the
parishes of Hampshire, and that they were further
extended to cover " evil behaviour in church 12d.
for every such offence."[5]   In 1571 all the churchwardens north of Hull and Chester underwent
searching enquiries about this division of their
work.   Not only were they asked if the fine had
been duly levied on defaulters, but also to give an
account of their stewardship for a year.   These
enquiries were reinforced by a strong injunction
commanding them to carry out the law, and in
addition the parish clergy were ordered to remind
their churchwardens of their duty in this respect
every Sunday in the middle of Morning Prayer.[6]

---

[1] *Second Ritual Report*, App. E., p. 403.
[2] *Guest MSS.*, vii. f. 98v (12).
[3] *State Papers Domestic*, xxxvi. 41 (14).
[4] Gee and Hardy, *Documents*, p. 473.
[5] *Horne MSS.*, f. 67 (12, 13).   This fine for bad behaviour in church was provided for by the Act of Uniformity.   This has been largely overlooked.   *Horne MS.*
affords the earliest evidence of this in actual parish life.
[6] *Second Ritual Report*, App. E., p. 407 (44); p. 411 (20).

In the same year the parishes of Cambridgeshire
were examined whether the fines for non-attendance
and bad behaviour had been levied; accounts were
asked of the monies received and lists of those who
refused to pay.[1]   A little later an order in almost
identical terms with that for Cambridgeshire was
enforced in London and the neighbourhood.[2]
In 1575 the parishes of Hampshire, Northern
Surrey and the Channel Islands received similar
commands,[3] and in 1576 the enquiries already referred to in connexion with the Northern counties
in 1571 were renewed.[4]   In 1583 Archbishop
Whitgift sent letters to all his brethren ordering
them to command their clergy to give warning
once a month in the parish churches that the Act
of Uniformity would be strictly enforced, and that
all churchwardens should furnish lists of nonconformists " fourteen days before each Sessions and
Assizes . . . . that the parties may be indicted
according to the statute."[5]   He also instituted an
enquiry himself in 1585 concerning remissness in
enforcing or collecting the fine " for absence from
Divine Service and unreverent behaviour thereat "
in the parishes of Sussex, and he further asked if
the clergy had carried out his order of 1583 with
regard to the warning in their churches, which, for
these parishes was changed—becoming weekly not
monthly.[6]   The severe statute of 1593 had its

---

[1] *Ibid.*, p. 406 (20).
[2] *British Museum Orders*, 698. h. 20 (10) [18]; *Guest
MSS.*, vii. f. 118 (21).
[3] *British Museum Orders*, 5155. de. 24 (37).
[4] Cardwell, *Annals*, i. 409.
[5] *Whitgift MS. Register*, i. f. 90v.   [6] *Ibid.*, f. 116v.

effect in this connexion. In the next year the Council wrote to Whitgift instructing him to gain information about all nonconforming Catholics in the parishes south of Hull and Chester, and the Archbishop issued orders that the clergy and churchwardens should make diligent enquiries and furnish lists of such nonconformists. It is interesting to note that special request was made for the names of Catholic women. Women during the reign were truer to the Faith than men.[1]

The evidence which we have quoted in such detail leaves no room for doubt that the laws against nonconformity were not allowed to fall into desuetude. It is clear that the parochial churchwardens were more than local officials. They formed a private information bureau in every parish, and their reports all through the reign found their way to the authorities. Thus, in every parish there existed an inquisitorial system—elaborated with care, and working uniformly for the purpose of enforcing the Elizabethan ideal in religion. There was little loophole for escape unless the churchwardens were dishonest, and broke the solemn oaths which they took on entering office. Had we admitted the evidence of local histories and of the account books of separate parishes, the proof could have been made overwhelming that there was no intermission in official vigilance. Sufficient documents, however, have been quoted to show that the imposition of fines for nonconformity was not left to the fitful caprice of the parochial authorities, but that the statute law was

[1] *Ibid.*, ii. f. 113.

imposed by the churchwardens with unceasing diligence, and that there was no relief in the parishes from their enquiries and reports.

Another feature of their work needs passing' mention. The documents to which we have already referred in this chapter provide us with an interesting insight into parochial behaviour at church. Talking, laughing, sleeping, fighting and even shedding of blood, inattention and mockery seem to have been common features of Elizabethan public worship. It was one thing to compel the people to come to church, it was quite another matter to make them believe that the new service was worthy of respect, or the new preaching worth listening to. There was a disposition—if we are to believe the manuscripts—to treat the Sunday services as fit subject for merriment, and to turn the parish church into either a parochial club, or a controversial meeting. Almost every document which we have used in referring to the duties of the churchwardens refers to the disgraceful behaviour of the parish congregations, and it is unnecessary to repeat the authorities. Efforts were made all along to bring about a better state of affairs, and the duty fell on the churchwardens. They stood like sentries waiting for disturbances, or they moved up and down the churches like policemen in a disturbed city area. Indeed in some places these efforts assumed appearances bordering on the absurd. In all the parishes of the large diocese of Coventry and Lichfield the clergy and churchwardens were ordered to choose eight, six, or four substantial, honest and able-bodied men in each parish who should take an oath to maintain order during the services. These " Orderlies " went round the church during public worship with " white rods in their hands." Disturbers were admonished to behave, and if they did not do so after one warning " the two honestest " of these chosen men " led them to the chancel door and set them with their faces looking towards the people for the space of a quarter of an hour."[1] In addition, in the same parishes a similar punishment was meted out to ale-wives and those who " tippled in the time of service."[2] It is not too much to say that public worship in Elizabethan parishes cannot have been edifying when it became necessary to resort to such expedients.

The third sphere in which the ideal was enforced was in the parish schools. The subject of Elizabethan education is largely unworked, and to consider its various aspects would lead us too far afield. It was a contemporary complaint that education during the period was neglected, and the Speaker of the House of Commons, in 1563, spoke of the want of schools and schoolmasters, and contrasted the ignorance of his own time with the flourishing condition of learning in the past.[3] In one respect, however, Elizabethan education excelled, and that was in the theological qualifications of the parish schoolmasters and in the minute care taken that the children should be well in-

[1] *State Papers Domestic*, xxxvi. 41 (13).
[2] *Ibid.* (15).
[3] Strype, *Annals*, I. i. 437. For the best survey of education in previous centuries see Rashdall, *Universities of Europe in the Middle Ages*; Leach, *English Schools of the Reformation*.

J

structed in the new religion.   Thus the coming
generation were brought up in sympathy with the
ideal from their earliest years.   The schoolmasters
were completely under the control of the bishops.
This arrangement, made by the Royal Injunctions,[1]
was reinforced by the Canons of 1571,[2] and was
confirmed by Act of Parliament in 1581.[3]   It
applied not merely to the ordinary parish teachers,
but to all private tutors.   They were carefully examined not so much with regard to their intellectual attainments as to their "right understand-
ing of God's true religion."   On their satisfying
this test they were given licences by the bishops
in writing under their seals.[4]   Their instruction
was regulated on a similar principle.   They were
forbidden to teach their scholars anything derogatory "to the religion now set forth by public
authority";[5] to use any books tending to such an
object, or "to propound to their scholars any
themes, vulgars, or subtle questions whereby
matters of religion, concluded or established, might
be made doubtful unto them, or they induced to
deride or scoff at any godly order, rite or ceremony
now set forth and allowed."[6] They were ordered
"to move and teach their children duly to reverence and love the true religion that is now set
forth . . . and to teach them such sentences out
of the Scripture as may frame them to godliness."[7]

[1] *Op. cit.*, No. 40.
[2] Church Historical Society, *op. cit.*, p. 82.
[3] 23 Eliz., c. i., 5.
[4] *E.g.*, *Rochester MSS.*, vii. f. 98 (19).
[5] *E.g.*, see *Second Ritual Report*, App. E., 411 (45).
[6] *British Museum Articles*, 5155. de. 24 (33).
[7] *Ibid.*, 5155. aa. 8 (44, 45).

But the Elizabethan parish schoolmasters' *vade mecum* was the *Primer*, which was a reformed edition of the lay-folks' service book of the Middle Ages, and was based on sound Protestant principles.[1] Schoolmasters were compelled to use this book as the bed rock of their religious teaching during the entire reign.[2] Indeed it survived in the schools of England until suppressed by Parliament in 1651. In addition, various *Catechisms* of the Reformed Religion in Latin or English were added to the parish school books from time to time. Whitgift's dealings with education illustrate perhaps better than anything else the care taken with regard to the teaching of the new religion. On Dec. 12, 1583, he issued the following orders to his brethren: " First, a general examination to be taken by the bishop in his province of all schoolmasters as well public as private, with order that such as are unsound may be removed . . Secondly, inquiry to be made how the children of the Recusants be brought up, and how many within their several dioceses, as well Recusants as others, have their children beyond the seas."[3] These regulations with regard to schoolmasters, school-religion, and Catholic children show how minutely the whole Elizabethan system was thought out. Teaching was entirely under the supervision of the new Episcopate, and this fact made it difficult for a Catholic or a Puritan to be a schoolmaster even in private.

[1] See reprint in *Private Prayers . . . reign of Queen Elizabeth* (Parker Society).
[2] *Royal Injunction of* 1559. No. 39.
[3] *Whitgift MS. Register*, i. f. 91 ; and see above, p. 112.

The religious instruction was carefully supervised and kept close to the Elizabethan standards of Protestantism, and the children of all those who were known to be out of sympathy with the system were reported to the Government.

Such then were the Elizabethan dealings with pious Catholic customs, the duties of church-wardens and parochial education. They help to fill in some details of the broad picture which we have surveyed in earlier chapters. The policy was destructive and constructive. Every link with the past was ruthlessly broken, so far as excessive vigilance could break it. Every effort was made by fines and penances to enforce attendance and attention at public worship. Every possible means was used to see that those who taught in the parishes were of unimpeachable Reformation orthodoxy, and that the parish children were cut off from anything Catholic and brought up in the strictest principles of the Established Church. These three aspects of parish life are then of more than passing importance. They represent the most matured methods of cutting the ties which bound the people to the past, and of laying Protestant foundations for the future. They illustrate the astuteness of Elizabethan zeal and the foresight of Elizabethan reform. To banish Catholic piety from the homes of the people, to allow only a Protestant form of worship, and to bring up the children in an atmosphere comparatively anti-Catholic, were the most subtle instruments used by the authorities to enforce their religious ideals.

CHAPTER IX.

SOME ASPECTS OF SOCIAL LIFE.

NO survey, however broad, of Elizabethan Parish Life, would be adequate without some consideration of the social conditions of the people. In this connexion our study must necessarily be short, and the point of view must be such as will include the greatest number of people and the most outstanding features. A closer study would lead into the spheres of Economics and Sociology, and would bring with it so much detail that it could not be handled with anything like proportion in a general study of Parish Life. In addition, social conditions were to a large extent in a transitional stage, and it is difficult in many aspects of them to find sufficient permanency to warrant the inclusion of them here. In this chapter then wide limitations must be accepted, and where departments of social life and conditions have not been touched on, or have been lightly referred to, difficulties have been avoided which would have overburdened the picture. Had these been included, the effect produced would have been too miscellaneous, and it has seemed best to attempt only certain features, and to keep the study as true to life within them as possible.[1]

The sixteenth century was one in which agricultural revolution held an important place. Broadly

[1] The general history must be read in the contemporary books; but all Mr. R. E. Prothero's writings on the subject are invaluable.

speaking, this revolution was the outcome of the
new age with its spirit of trade and commerce.
In relation to the land, this spirit can be traced
in the development of enclosures, which led to the
complete destruction of the communistic spirit of
the Middle Ages, and applied the individualism of
the new era to the land. Competitive life in every
sphere of human activity overturned the old parish
partnerships in land, and the individual owner
gradually appeared in place of the older institution of common parochial ownership. The history
of this change can be traced for many years beyond
our period. What chiefly concerns us is that lands
which had been used for agricultural purposes
were transformed into grazing lands, that sheep-
farming took the place of grain-growing, and that
wool became a more valuable asset than corn or
cattle. Thus ideals changed. Under the old
régime, landlords used their lands to maintain men
for national or private service; under the new com-
mercial conditions, they looked on land as an aid
to wealth. This change produced a corresponding
effect on the people who rented and worked farms.
Their fathers did not see in the soil much beyond
their livelihood, the new Tudor generation imitated
their predecessors, and worked to make money from
it as well. Land was commercialized. The result
was a complete revolution. Community of interests
in the supply of necessities gave place to individual
enterprize in the struggle for wealth, and as the
demand for wool increased, agriculture declined
before the wide provision of sheep-farms. How
this change was brought about in actual life does

not concern us. There was doubtless much dishonesty and much suffering. Influence and money
played their part in the break-up, nor were the
advantages of mutual give-and-take overlooked.
The fact, however, that the changes took place is
sufficient for our survey. It can easily be seen
that serious parochial results followed. Not merely
was the old communistic ideal destroyed, but the
disappearance of agricultural pursuits slowly but
surely alienated the people in the country parishes
from the land, and small agricultural farmers disappeared before the ever-widening sweep of sheep
enclosures. In addition, other types of farm
workers were placed under serious disadvantages
—the ploughman, the sower, the reaper, the
teamster disappeared before the general demand
for a comparatively small number of men as shep-
herds, in a labour market now increased by many
unemployed. Wool was an easy and safe way to at
any rate a moderate fortune. The market was
secure. Had it been possible to continue agricultural pursuits, they were at best precarious and
fluctuating in the new struggle for money. Sheep
were a cheap source of gain, and tillage lands,
cottages, barns and such like made way for wide
and unbroken areas of pasture. Efforts were made
at times to prevent the depopulation of the parishes,
and to control the system of enclosures, but for the
first half of the reign sheep farming advanced to
the detriment of a large population in the rural
parishes. Later a reaction set in—too many enclosures had glutted the markets with English wool,
and its value gradually declined, and at this point

Parliament stepped in to forbid the turning of any land that remained under agriculture into grazing lands, and to order the re-conversion of a large portion of the new grazing lands into tillage. The preamble of the Act[1] provides an interesting contemporary comment on the state of affairs: " Whereas the strength and flourishing estate of this kingdom is greatly upheld and advanced by the maintenance of the plough and tillage, being the occasion of the increase and multiplying of people both for service in the wars and times of peace, being also a principal means that the people are set at work and thereby drawn from idleness, drunkenness, unlawful games and other lewd practices, and whereas by the same means the greater part of the subjects are preserved from extreme poverty and the wealth of the realm is kept dispersed and distributed in many hands, where it is more ready to answer all necessary charges, for the services of the realm; and whereas also the said husbandry and tillage is a cause that the realm doth stand more upon itself without depending upon foreign countries for either bringing in of corn in time of scarcity, or for vent and utterance of our own commodities being in over great abundance . . . and whereas there have grown up many depopulations by turning tillage into pasture . . . . . be it enacted," &c. Perhaps no one suffered more from the changes than the labourer who formed no small part of the rural population. Not only was his sphere of work largely curtailed, but his wages, fixed by an Act of Parliament a

[1] 39 and 40 Eliz., c. ii.

century old, bore no proper relationship to the increased cost of living. The market was overstocked as never before, and unemployment increased on all sides. On the other hand, where agriculture continued, less and less labour was employed in connexion with it. The land became worn out as men forgot almost everything of the science of farming which had been fostered in the country by the skill of the monastic landlords, and consequently less labour was employed. However, efforts were made in not a few directions to bring about a better state of affairs. Books on agriculture began to appear, and although they were somewhat primitive in their suggestions, yet they did something to stem the flowing tide of ignorance in agriculture. In addition, in the Southern and Eastern counties there were many successful attempts made at market-gardening; but conditions generally went from bad to worse until, as we have seen, the value of wool decreased. A miniature reaction then set in, and the produce of the land increased in value. On all sides the conditions of life improved. Agriculture advanced, and this advance was along newer lines. Indeed the system of enclosures seems in the long run to have benefited agriculture, and contemporary evidence goes to prove that in many of the parishes —especially in the South and East—the enclosed pasture lands produced the best crops. Of course, the gentry uniformly profited, but the reaction helped the farmers. They lived in well-furnished houses and Elizabethan writers noted their prosperity. This arose not so much from any sudden

advance in methods—which remained deplorably
inadequate during the reign—but from the increase
of prices, and from the laws which fixed the wages
of labour at miserable rates.

Thus then, in connexion with the land, the
parishes of Elizabethan England went through a
period of storm and stress not unlike that connected
with their religion. As a rule, the gentry and
larger farmers prospered, but the burden of change
fell on the smaller holders and on the agricultural
labourers. Parochial poverty was one of the
characteristics of the reign, and became an ever-
increasing problem. In 1563 an elaborate Act[1]
for relief of the poor was passed, which expanded
in a stringent way a Marian Statute[2] dealing with
the same subject. This Act is most important, as
it regulated poor relief according to parishes.
Collectors were appointed in every parish, and it
became more difficult to refuse the appointment,
as the fine was raised for such refusal to £10, which
the churchwardens could recover by legal process; and if they failed in this duty, they themselves were liable to a fine of £20. Dishonesty
was discouraged among the parish collectors, by
changing the punishment from ecclesiastical censure to imprisonment. A complete register of all
parishioners was ordered, and those who were able
to give must support their parish poor by weekly
subscriptions, at their own rate, gathered by the
collectors at the Sunday service and entered
opposite the names in the parish register. Con-

[1] 5 Eliz., c. i.
[2] 2 and 3 Philip and Mary, c. v.

tributions were compulsory, and obstinate refusal after gentle admonitions was punished by imprisonment. If the contributions of rural parishes were insufficient to support the parish poor, permission was granted to the local justices to grant licences for begging on the recommendation of the clergyman and two or three of the principal inhabitants. In cities and towns provision was made for such contingencies by arranging that the wealthier parishes should help their less fortunate neighbours. Spite of legislation, poverty increased and vagabonds became a nuisance up and down the country. Unsuccessful attempts were made at legislation in 1571,[1] but in the following year an Act was passed which dealt with vagabondage and poverty.[2] All " rogues, vagabonds and sturdy beggars " above the age of sixteen were on conviction " grievously whipped and burnt through the gristle of the right ear with a hot iron of the compass of an inch about." This punishment could only be escaped by the willingness of someone to take the convicted person into service for a year; and it was duly carried out if such service was not persevered in. After punishment—either by whipping and burning or a year's service—if the vagabond relapsed, he was put to death as a felon. The statutory definition of a vagabond provides an excellent illustration of the various types abroad during the period: " idle persons using subtle, crafty and unlawful games and some of them feigning themselves to have knowledge in physiog-

[1] D'Ewes, *Journal*, 165.   [2] 13 Eliz., c. v.

nomy, palmistry, or other abused sciences, and all persons being whole and mighty in body and able to labour, having not land or master nor using any lawful merchandise craft or mystery;[1] and all fencers, bearwards, common players in interludes and minstrels not belonging to any baron of this realm or towards any other honourable personage of greater degree; all jugglers, tinkers, pedlars and petty chapmen . . and all common labourers being persons able in body and using loitering, and refusing to work for such reasonable wages as is taxed and commonly given; and all counterfeiters of licences, passports and all users of the same, knowing the same to be counterfeited; and all scholars of the Universities of Oxford and Cambridge that go about begging not being authorized under the seal of the said Universities; and all shipmen pretending losses by sea, other than such as shall be hereafter provided for; and all persons delivered out of gaols that beg for their fees, not having licences, shall be deemed rogues, vagabonds and sturdy beggars." The list affords the best contemporary summary of the various nuisances who infested the country. In addition, poor relief was placed on a securer basis. The amount of the weekly subscription was no longer left to the discretion of each parishioner. An estimate was made of the amount necessary for the support of the parish poor, and the well-to-do inhabitants were assessed at a weekly charge sufficient to cover the estimated annual expenditure. An appeal was allowed to the Sessions, but if the assessment was

[1] " Ministerium "—trade.

upheld imprisonment followed. Alms-houses were
provided and a regular monthly examination was
held of the poor maintained in them, and those who
did not belong to the parish were sent to their
native parishes. As the reign advanced further
legislation took place. In 1576, the experiment
was made of making the poor work. The collectors
in each parish provided raw materials out of the
weekly collections and these were worked up by the
poor who were paid at the collectors' estimate " of
the desert of the work done "—the work being sold
in the market. Refusal to do such work was
punishable in a " house of correction "—where
" irons " and " whips " were characteristic features.
In the last Parliament of the reign statutes[1] were
passed amplifying previous regulations by providing that children or parents must relieve their
needy friends. The severe penalties on vagabonds
were, however, mitigated.[2]

When we turn to the ecclesiastical documents we
find that many efforts were made to bring the
Elizabethan Poor Laws into close contact with
parochial life. Indeed the parish church was the
natural centre for the enforcing of such regulations,
as the statutory collections were made there, and the
churchwardens were intimately connected with the
administration of the laws. In the county of
Norfolk in 1569,[3] the churchwardens were asked
to furnish returns dealing with the legal collections

[1] 39 Eliz., c. iii. and iv.
[2] The best account of the Poor Laws is in Miss E. M.
Leonard's *Early History of English Poor Law Relief*
(1900).
[3] *Second Ritual Report*, App. E., p. 404.

and distribution of alms. In the same year this
enquiry was extended to certain parishes in Kent,[1]
and carelessness about the appointment of collectors was reproved in the counties of Gloucester
and Worcester.[2] In the Northern parishes of
England, in Cambridgeshire and in the London
parishes, the legal regulations were strictly enforced in 1571,[3] and the local collectors were compelled to hand in written quarterly returns to the
parish clergymen and churchwardens. At the
same time orders were issued to avoid fraud and
deceit in the administration of the funds, and to
furnish detailed lists of those who refused to pay
their poor-dues. In Northern Kent[4] similar orders
were given in the following year, but the accounts
were annual, not quarterly. The refusal to sub-
scribe under the Acts was severely looked into.
In the parishes of Norfolk[5] returns of such de-
linquents were demanded in 1561, and in Kent in
1569.[6] This enquiry was extended over a wider
number of parishes in a more searching form in
1572,[7] and in addition the names of those who
encouraged others to break the law were called
for in Middlesex. Parallel with the enforcement
of these statutes in the parishes, other regulations
were at work. A non-resident clergyman was compelled by frequent episcopal orders to give a

---

[1] *Parker MS. Register*, i. f. 320.
[2] *Lansdowne MSS.*, xi. f. 204.
[3] *Second Ritual Report*, App. E., pp. 406, 407, 411;
and *Brit. Museum Articles*, 698. h. 20 (10).
[4] *Rochester MSS.*, vii. f. 128v.
[5] *Brit. Museum Articles*, 5155. aa. 8 (1).
[6] *Parker Register, op. cit.*
[7] *Ritual Report, op. cit.*

fortieth part of his income to the relief of the poor
in his parish. This regulation was enforced from
1559 to the close of the reign.[1] The people were
diligently instructed from time to time to give to
the poor such sums as they were accustomed to
provide " for popish worship and religion "; while
the fines for not coming to the parish church on
Sundays were collected by the churchwardens and
distributed among the needy together with the
regular parochial subscriptions. These customs
were common to all the parishes and continued
throughout Elizabeth's reign.[2] Parochial poverty
was a serious problem, and the various efforts made
to relieve it by both the Government and the Established Church affected the details of parish church
in a marked degree. It is interesting to note that
while the change of religion did not divorce poor
relief from religious associations, yet it required
Acts of Parliament to help the new Church's
efforts, and it laid the burden of carrying out the
additional work on the clergy and churchwardens.
Elizabeth and her advisers were always generous
with other people's money and labour.

The various social degrees were as a rule fairly
represented in most of the parishes. The Queen
made frequent progresses throughout the country
with large retinues, and as a consequence the nobles
kept up magnificent establishments which reflected
the somewhat dazzling life of the Court. They
lived, however, mostly in London, and the gentry

[1] See Strype, *Annals*, I. ii., App. xxi., *British Museum
Articles*, 5155. de. 24 (1575); *Whitgift MS. Register*,
i. ff. 145, 149 (1596).

[2] For examples see Strype and *Ritual Report, op. cit.*

in the parishes were usually men of moderate fortunes who lived quietly in the country following rural pursuits, and leading a life somewhat like that of the country gentleman of to-day. Their wives and daughters aped Court fashions as far as possible, and these passed down—modified as to-day by financial considerations—through the parson's wife to the lower grades of parochial society. The middle classes were gradually growing up throughout the country, and the lines of distinction between them and the lower classes were becoming more defined. On the other hand, the divisions were not marked as to-day by rigid regulations. In the country especially there was much freedom of intercourse between all classes, and a general atmosphere of good fellowship. Even the poor were admitted at times into the common parish enjoyments where the squire, the parson, the lawyer, the doctor, the farmer, and the labourer met together, and forgot for a time the storm and stress of Elizabethan life. Indeed enjoyment was a characteristic note of the age. The Queen's ruling passion was pleasure, and this affected the national outlook. Gaiety was the most outstanding feature of Court life, and this excessive pursuit of amusement introduced manners—coarse, flippant, suggestive and gross. Other grades of society reflected the Court's enthusiasm for pleasure and the decay of the Court's manners. Lack of refinement was common in every social circle, and the uneducated imitated the examples of their social superiors, and considered the unedifying life of the Court as the proper expression of the highest education. This ceaseless round of gaiety produced extravagance in dress. The Queen went to the extremes of vanity, and the people followed suit according to their means. Indeed Elizabethan women felt so much the influence of their monarch's appearance, that they ate ashes and tallow to acquire the royal paleness of cheeks, and they enclosed themselves in the tightest dresses to imitate the slenderness of the royal figure. High and low did their utmost in this respect. The gentry vied with one another in ornamental dress—even wearing bracelets and earrings and using perfumes. Fashions changed with as much rapidity as to-day, and the squire of 1559 was as differently dressed from the squire of 1570 or 1603 as his modern descendant from his immediate ancestors. Even the clergy did not escape the prevailing custom. In many instances they cast aside the legal outdoor dress—" a square cap and cloak for walking, and a long gown and hat for riding as became sober and discreet ministers "—and appeared in public in fantastic dress such as the gentry affected. Indeed observers were not slow to note that everywhere dress was an Elizabethan craze, which was indulged by all classes in spite of legal regulations to restrain and direct it.[1] With regard to the dress of the poor little evidence is forthcoming, but the little information which has survived goes to prove that no radical changes had taken place.

[1] See a Royal Proclamation of Feb. 12, 1566, in Strype, *Annals*, I. ii. App. xxxiv., which confirmed the Henrician statute against excess in dress (24 Henry VIII., c. xiii.), and certain clauses of a Marian statute dealing with the same subject (1 and 2 Philip and Mary, c. ii.).

K

Country life was enlivened by hunting and shooting, bear-baiting, wrestling, football, and travelling shows provided amusement for the people in general. Various festivals had sports peculiar to themselves. Dancing and card-playing were indulged in during the winter. At Easter, travelling companies provided plays at night, while cockfights whiled away the day, varied by rustic games and the morris dance. May Day had its old amusements, when Lords of Misrule even invaded the parish churches, and thus called forth stringent restrictions.[1]   In addition, various enjoyments connected with the harvest still survived, and the churchwardens were not averse to raising funds for parochial objects by selling beer at " church ales." Each parish had its own annual festival, and births, deaths, and marriages furnished occasions for much coarse feasting and drinking. The people were excessive eaters, though they had only two meals a day, and home brewed beer was drunk in abundance. Among the upper classes the meals were inconceivably luxurious to modern ears. The poor ate little bread and indulged largely in vegetable diet, varied with meat at festivals. The whole social life of the parishes was actuated by one spirit— self-indulgence, and things went so far that the services in the church were often disturbed by the playing of bowls, and dice and cards. Indeed Sunday amusements became so common that the

[1] See *Second Ritual Report*, App. E., p. 412; Stubbs, *Anatomie of Abuses* (New Shaks. Soc.), p. 147; and *British Museum Articles*, 5155. de. 24 (1).

bishops were compelled to step in, and to issue severe injunctions against them.[1] Doubtless the taverns encouraged Sunday sports, as episcopal orders had to be issued closing them at least during divine service.[2] There was much shopping on Sundays and holydays, and the Sunday evenings were given to dancing and gaming much to the disgust of the episcopate. Amusement had got out of hand in the general loosening of religious principles.

The agricultural changes, the dealings with the poor, and the necessity for controlling pleasure provided no small amount of anxiety to the authorities. Social conditions were in no very enviable state, and there was abroad a spirit of irresponsibility which took its origin in Court life and affected every part of the country. The growth of Puritanism helped to emphasize this spirit. The people had lost much of the old national self-control, and in not a few instances they accentuated their pleasures out of spite at the growth of severer views of life. Of course, there were many men of staid and disciplined character, but, broadly speaking, the predominant note in social life was one of unrestrained desire to get and provide enjoyment.[3] Much as contemporary Puritan pamphlets are to be discounted in their surveys of this subject, yet they contain many observations

[1] See orders of 1573 in *Rochester MSS.*, vii. f. 128v.
[2] For such prohibitions see *Second Ritual Report*, App. E., p. 408.
[3] See Harrison, *Description of England*; Rye, *England . . . in the reign of Elizabeth and James I.*; Strutt, *Dress and Habits of the People of England*, and *Sports and Pastimes.*

which cannot be lightly overlooked, and if they erred in asking severe measures, it is only too true that they were dealing with great excesses in every sphere of social life. The moral condition of the country, to which we shall refer later, reflected the national temperament.

CHAPTER X.

GRAVE AND GAY.

WE have considered some of the duties of the churchwardens, especially with regard to fines for nonconformity and to behaviour in church. Several other aspects of parochial life are also intimately connected with their work, and can best be considered in relation to it. The most important of these related to the local courts and to parochial finance, and included the superintendence of parochial morality.[1] The state of morality in the Elizabethan parishes can be summed up as unsatisfactory. The records present a picture on which we would do well not to gaze too long. At the same time we cannot completely pass it by. Before attempting to sum up, even in a broad manner, the moral conditions of the age, an obvious criticism must be met. It is not customary to judge the morality of a country or a city or a parish purely

---

[1] Mr. Ware's little book on parochial finance and administration under Elizabeth is full of suggestive material. As I have written of it elsewhere: " He deserves great praise for his little work . . . we have an excellent and readable picture of the ecclesiastical and financial side of parochial finance and government in Elizabethan England " (*English Historical Review*, xxiv. p. 405).

by its criminal statistics, and it follows that an estimate of parochial life ought not to depend solely on such evidence. It must at once be conceded that normally this is a just criticism. On the other hand, when the criminal records of any defined area are consistently bad, and when no improvement is seen over a number of years, we can conclude that life in that area is stagnant and unwholesome. In addition, when the records disclose not only that morality shows no improvement, but a uniform tendency to get worse; when criminal cases increase from year to year, we are justified in accepting such records as an unmistakable indication of the state of morality in the area under consideration. Such a position would be strengthened if we found it hard to discover any appearance of a healthy parochial opinion, or if the general tone of parochial opinion was unwholesome and decadent. All these conditions are fulfilled in Elizabethan times. The parochial and diocesan records disclose a consistency of moral decay in all classes of society which can hardly be paralleled in English history—the general gloom is only lit up here and there by individual characters —and it is almost impossible to find a sufficient number of parishes in such a good moral condition as to warrant their life being taken into consideration. There was no general religious conviction if we except Puritans and Catholics, and as a consequence there was little moral restraint.[1] Within

[1] Compare Dr. Frere: " The practice of religion had sunk to a very low ebb as the standard of decency in worship and efficiency in clerical ministration had gone down. There had been a moment when hatred of Spain and

our limits it is impossible to elaborate the proof
of this statement in detail. Two sources of evidence may, however, be referred to, as they cover
such wide areas and are extended over the entire
reign. The Episcopal Visitations in the various
parishes contain consistent requests for the names
of moral offenders, and the injunctions issued by
the ecclesiastical authorities against immorality in
the parishes are painful in their repetition throughout the whole period. It must be remembered that
Episcopal Visitation injunctions were issued after
searching questions had been seriously submitted
to the clergy, churchwardens and laity, and that
they were based on the answers received to such
questions. These praiseworthy injunctions failed
to produce reform. Personal character requires
more than public inquisition and the application
of legal remedies. It is significant that in all the
episcopal documents there are no references to
confession. The Elizabethan bishops do not appear
to have approved even of the spirit of the New
Service Book; for in all their enquiries dealing
with the clergy and the sick, they merely order
the clergyman to use " comfortable words of
Scripture " and enjoin him to see that wills contained no bequests for " popish superstitions." The
rubric providing for auricular confession during
sickness had evidently been stillborn, as the bishops,
while sweeping the Prayer Book as a source for

Rome seemed to be the only bit of religion left in the
English Church " (*Church under Elizabeth and James I.*,
p. 284); and Hubert Hall " The state of society was the
worst that had ever before been in the land " (*Society in
the Elizabethan Age*, p. 105).

enquiries, uniformly omitted all mention of it.
Again, the records of the ecclesiastical courts
abound in presentations for moral offences. If we
discount these presentations by fifty per cent., to
cover corruption on the part of officials, we may
certainly weaken the evidence for moral slackness
in the parishes; but at the same time we open up
spheres of corruption in the administration which
have almost baffled the imagination of historians.[1]
The general atmosphere of parochial life was so
unhealthy, and the stronger elements in parish life
had so much to do to keep themselves from in-
fection that their influence for good was little felt.
The bishops were avaricious, the parochial clergy,
as we have seen, fell far short of their calling,
and the administration of local government was
deplorably corrupt. Purity, honesty, fair dealing,
and justice do not flourish under such conditions.

The archdeacon's court was the normal centre
for parochial rule. It was held—half-yearly as
a rule—in the parish church of some large town
or village, and its jurisdiction covered all the
parishes in the archdeaconry. Previous warning
was given in each parish when the court would
open, and the churchwardens drew up their lists of
presentations for the presiding archdeacon. As
regards the churchwardens themselves, they had,
in addition to giving an account of their work with
regard to conformity and church behaviour, to in-
form the archdeacon of the state of their church
ornaments, and of the suitability of their churches

---

[1] See J. F. Stephen: *History of Criminal Law*, ii. 413,
on the corrupt state of the Elizabethan Courts.

for public worship. The records provide us with some diligent inquisitions in this connexion which at times are not devoid of humour. Thus the presiding officer might not be convinced that the necessary books were provided, and the parish Bible and Prayer Book had to be produced in court and the parish had to pay the expense; or a representative had to ride to a city to see if a Bible which had been found belonged to his parish, and the blacksmith's charges for shoeing his horse on the journey appear in the parish account book. Surplices also were brought to court, and when these were found " very indecent," the archdeacon told the churchwardens that they had broken their oaths, and ordered them to confess their fault before the congregation and to provide proper garments for the minister.[1] Failure in such duties as these brought the churchwardens within the merciless meshes of the notorious chicanery of the courts; for relief from penances could only be obtained by satisfying the various professional court-fees. Nor were the churchwardens alone at the mercy of such exactions. An entire parish might find itself placed under ecclesiastical ban for neglecting to obey the orders of the courts. Before church privileges were restored the parish had to pay exorbitant fees to the ecclesiastical officials in addition to all the travelling expenses of their representatives and, at times, the outlay for liquid refreshment for the bishop or archdeacon.[2]

[1] Cf. W. H. Hale, *Series of Precedents*, &c., pp. 170 ff.

[2] Cf. *Transactions Shropshire Historical Society*, i. 62.

The churchwardens also kept a close eye on the parish clergyman. The ritual and ceremonial which he employed were carefully watched as well as his moral character. If he refused to wear a surplice, they reported him to the court, and received orders not merely to see that the surplice was in the parish vestry before the service, but to take it with them into the church, and to go up to the minister and offer it to him before the assembled congregation. If he still refused to wear it, he was summoned to the court on the churchwardens' presentment for punishment.[1] Indeed the parson's private and public life was at the mercy of such inquisitions, and on occasions the parish officials adhered so closely to the letter of the law that they carried out the royal injunction already referred to with regard to clerical marriage, and reported their clergyman because they were not certain whether his wife had passed the legally proscribed examination before the magistrates previous to her marriage, and whether he had been duly licenced to marry.[2] His general unfitness for office might be summarily complained of under the charge " we are not edified by him."[3] The clergyman, however, had ample opportunity for hitting back, as, according to legal regulation, he was ordered to supervise the churchwardens and report on their personal and public conduct;[4] so there was much give-and-take in parochial

[1] Cf. *Lancashire Antiquarian Society's Transactions*, xiii. 59.

[2] Cf. *Yorkshire Archaeological Journal*, xviii. 320.

[3] Cf. Hale, p. 159.

[4] Cf. *Ritual Report*, App. E., p. 411 (20).

government.   In addition it was the parson's duty
to see that the archdeacon's excommunication
against anyone was carried out.   He read it from
the parish pulpit, inhibited the culprit from parish
worship, and read the form of confession for him
to repeat before the assembled congregation, when
he sought release from the sentence.   On such
an occasion he preached on the sin or offence in
question, and pointed the moral from the predica-
ment of the offender.[1]

But the archdeacons' courts had a much wider
sphere of influence than in such matters as have
been referred to.   They brought pressure to bear
on the pockets of the people if they refused to pay
their appointed parochial rates.   The smallest
details did not escape detection.   Thus if a half-
penny a week to the poor box was considered too
small a contribution, the churchwardens resented
such narrow charity and it was lucky if the excuse
" not so wealthy as men taketh him to be " served
the defendant before the judge.[2]   Indeed it may
be said that parish life in the majority of its
activities came under the local government of the
archdeacons' courts.   The question naturally arises :
How did these courts ensure that their sentences or
orders would be properly carried out?   Threats,
repeated injunctions, irritating and ceaseless sum-
monses to the courts were all at the disposal of the
officials in their efforts to make local government
practicable, but the greatest power was undoubtedly

[1] Cf. Hale, pp. 160, 206; *Archaeologia Cantiana*, xxvii.
219; Cardwell, *Synodalia*, i. 155.
[2] Hale, p. 149.

that of excommunication—either greater or lesser. The former cut off a culprit from participation in public worship and the sacraments, the latter turned him into a social outcast and virtually ostracised him. It may appear strange that excommunication should be given such prominence as a means for enforcing the orders and regulations of the courts in an age when religion was little better than obedience to an Act of Parliament. The records, however, prove that no stronger power belonged to local administration. A man under excommunication dare not marry, and if he did he was liable to severe penance.[1] If he entered church he was either removed by the churchwardens or the service had to be abandoned.[2] Greater excommunication destroyed a culprit's business, as any communications or dealings with him were indictable offences. He could not give evidence on oath. If he sued in court the defendant could produce evidence that he stood an unabsolved suitor and a non-suit immediately resulted. In addition, the process of restoration to religious and civil rights was fenced round by costly procedure. Absolution from excommunication was an expensive business in an Elizabethan court. Nor was the local court baffled by obstinacy. The Court of High Commission took cognizance of such an offence and had at its command both heavy fines and severe imprisonments. Finally, the bishop could certify the offence to the Queen in Chancery, who on the bishop's *significavit* issued a writ *De*

[1] Cf. Hale, p. 223.
[2] *Ibid.*, p. 198.

excommunicato capiendo to the county sheriff, and the offender was lodged in the county gaol until reconciled to the church.[1] Excommunication involved other difficulties for a defaulter. He was liable to be fined for not attending public worship, and he could not plead his sentence as an excuse—while he was liable to further mulct for not having his excommunication legally removed. Excommunication hung over the head of anyone who disobeyed the local courts in any respect, and when it was pronounced, its removal involved under any circumstances a costly process. It was not only difficult to escape from the long arm of the law, but it was comparatively easy to come within its reach. The local courts could proceed by oath *ex officio*, and as a result of the merest gossip anyone might be compelled to swear away his own character. Anyone might carry a report to the local parish officials against his neighbour, and on presentation the minutest details of private life could be extorted on oath. Guilty and innocent alike were caught in the net of court fees and legal expenses. Parochial life then, from the point of view of local government, was not enviable. The whole system tended to produce trickery, corruption, false witnesses, and hypocrisy. Even if we could accept a fairer view of it, the fact that juries did not exist in the local courts rendered the proof of innocence

---

[1] Stephens, *Commentaries on the Laws of England*, iii. 349-350 (12th edn.). Compare *Whitgift MS. Register*, i. f. 90v. Whitgift ordered that stubborn Catholics should be excommunicated, "and if they stood in excommunication forty days [the bishops] should procure the writ *De excommunicato capiendo* against them."

exceedingly difficult.   The ordinary presumption
of innocence did not apply. The accused frequently
could not afford to produce witnesses-on-oath to
swear that his denial of the charge against him
was true, and sentence was thus pronounced against
him by default.   Contemporary complaints against
both procedure and corruption failed to produce
reform, and parochial life during the reign remained at the mercy of a cumbersome system of
local government in which abuses were more
common than either honesty or justice.

Finally, the churchwardens were responsible for
the financial affairs of the parish.   It is unnecessary
to consider parish endowments, as they are an
obvious source of income. Fines for nonconformity,
for refusal to contribute to the poor, and at times
a regular parish rate on households, helped to re-
plenish the parochial purse.   The fees for baptisms, marriages, burials, and, in places, rents from
pews also provided ways and means. But parochial
church-ales were the most popular method of
raising money both with the churchwardens and
people.   These were held annually at stated inter-
vals and the extant churchwardens' accounts prove
that they were as a rule a financial success.   Frequently an extraordinary church-ale was held in a
parish and invitations were issued to several neighbouring parishes, and these were read after the
sermon on Sundays from the pulpits of the parishes
thus honoured.   These gatherings lasted a week
or more, and vast supplies of food and ale soon
disappeared amid the general conviviality.   Excessive drinking was looked upon with approval,

and the more ale a man could consume the wider reputation would he gain for godliness and charity.[1]   Church-ales did not tend to improve morality, and as they were the constant object of attack from the Puritan party, they gradually disappeared to make room for parochial games and stage plays.   The churchwardens frequently organized these on a large scale, and turned them into sources of income by collections or charges for admission.   Many other expedients were resorted to, and the general impression left by their history is one of insecurity in parochial finance.

Parish life under Queen Elizabeth was in no healthy state.   Lack of respect for authority was evident in clerical life, and in the parish services. Religious differences were accentuated by penal laws.   Moral standards did not exist.   The entire local government was honeycombed with abuses. There was no such thing as privacy.   Spying was not only common but was encouraged.   Education was in the widest sense neglected.   Genuine religion was so uncommon as to be almost negligible. A general irresponsibility characterized the various grades of society.   It is almost impossible to find anything to praise, and much, which space has excluded, remains for blame.   Whatever may be said of Elizabethan England in its relation to nationality, foreign affairs, and literature, it must be confessed that the state of parish life was deplorable. To the Catholic missionaries, fired with enthusiasm,

[1] Cf. Stubbs, *op. cit.*, p. 110.

England presented a pitiable picture of moral anarchy: "religion had been going from bad to worse . . . the churches were profaned and closed, piety was decayed, and a gloom of spiritual apathy had settled over the land."[1] To the honest Puritan at home the parishes of England were little better than heathen. The Elizabethan ideal of national religious unity failed in its own day because it neglected the true foundations of character. Subsequent history proves that it was a failure, because we can trace to it the blood-stained scaffold at Whitehall, and because to the long winter of Catholic repression succeeded the beauties of the Second Spring.

[1] Dr. Frere, *op. cit.*, p. 208.

FINIS.

INDEX.

—

L

THE CATHOLIC LIBRARY

ONE SHILLING NET EACH VOLUME.

(Postage 2½d.)

ALREADY PUBLISHED

VOL. 1.

Letters and Instructions of St. Ignatius Loyola, vol. I.

VOLS. 2 and 4.

A Defence of English Catholics. By William Allen, afterwards Cardinal. With a Preface by His Eminence the Cardinal Archbishop of Westminster (2 vols.).

VOL. 3.

S. Antonino and Mediæval Economics. By the Rev. Bede Jarrett, O.P.

VOLS. 5 and 7.

Holy Mass: The Eucharistic Sacrifice and the Roman Liturgy. By the Rev. Herbert Lucas, S.J. (2 vols.)

VOL. 6.

Campion's Ten Reasons. (The original Latin text, with a translation by the Rev. Joseph Rickaby, S.J., and an historical Introduction by the Rev. John Hungerford Pollen, S.J.

VOL. 8.

The Triumphs over Death. By the Ven. Robert Southwell, poet and martyr. Together with three famous letters by the same. Edited by J. W. Trotman.

VOL. 9.

Parish Life in the Reign of Queen Elizabeth. By W. P. M. Kennedy, M.A. (Dublin and Oxon), F.R. Hist. S., Professor of History at the University, Antigonish, Nova Scotia.

THE CATHOLIC LIBRARY

ONE SHILLING NET EACH VOLUME

(Postage 2½d.)

IN THE PRESS

VOL. 10.

The Religious Poems of Crashaw. A Study and a Selection. By R. A. Eric Shepherd.

VOL. 11.

S. Bernardino of Siena, the People's Preacher: with selections from his sermons. By Miss Maisie Ward.

VOL. 12.

Lourdes. By the Very Rev. Mgr. R. H. Benson, M.A.

VOL. 13.

The Question of Miracles. By the Rev. G. H. Joyce, S.J., Professor of Dogmatic Theology at St. Beuno's College, N. Wales.

VOL. 14.

Commentary on the Seven Penitential Psalms. By the Blessed John Fisher. Edited by J. S. Phillimore, M.A., Professor of Latin at Glasgow University.

VOL. 15.

Some Thoughts on Catholic Apologetics. A Plea for Interpretation. By Edward Ingram Watkin, M.A. (New College, Oxford).

VOL. 16.

Catholic Hymnody. An historical survey of the great hymn-writers of the Church from the earliest times. By Joseph Clayton, M.A.

LONDON:

THE MANRESA PRESS, ROEHAMPTON, S.W.
B. HERDER, 68, GREAT RUSSELL ST., W.C.